7572

THE LIVING NOVEL

THE
LIVING

EDITED BY GRANVILLE HICKS

NOVEL:

a symposium

The Macmillan Company : New York : 1957

Contents

v

Contents

vi

Foreword

THIS BOOK is dedicated to the proposition that the novel is important, and is addressed to a skeptical world. That the contributors believe in the importance of the novel they have demonstrated in the best possible way—by learning how to write good novels and by writing them. Some have been reasonably well rewarded for their efforts, while others have been the despair of successive publishers, but they have all gone on writing with seriousness and devotion. If, for the sake of this book, they have taken time from the writing of fiction to set down their reflections on some of the problems of the novelist and of the novel, that is because they feel that these problems are urgent. Today the serious novel is both attacked and neglected, often enough by the same individuals. The serious novelist does his work in an atmosphere of confusion and hostility, and though he probably should resist the temptation to strike back at the enemies of the novel,* he may legitimately seek to dispel misunderstanding.

* What I mean by this phrase is explained in the Afterword.

Foreword

The idea that there should be such a book grew out of the distress I felt on reading one more pronouncement—it doesn't matter whose—on the death of the novel. I was not merely distressed; I was puzzled. I believed, and believe, that there have never been so many serious novelists at work in America as there are in this period; I am not talking about great novelists, who are rare enough in any age, but about men and women who believe in the novel, who write out of themselves and not for the market, who recognize that there is a craft to be mastered and are determined to master it, and who have already made it clear that they have talent enough to warrant their ambitions.

How, then, could I explain this solemn assertion, repeated every few weeks by somebody or other, that the novel was dying if not quite dead? I could only assume that, while the writers of serious fiction were multiplying, something was happening to the readers and potential readers of such fiction. There were not only the literati* who said smugly that they couldn't read contemporary novels; there were also the intelligent but preoccupied men and women of my acquaintance who said unhappily that they didn't. I knew of serious novels of substantial merit that had been almost completely neglected by the reviewers and had had only a few hundred readers. Many people, people who ought to know better, were acting as if the serious novel were expendable. "Well, well," I could imagine them saying whenever another eminent authority reported that the novel had passed away, "What a relief!"

If there seemed no point in arguing with the supercilious pundits, it might, I thought, be possible to speak to those whose neg-

* "I can read the later Joyce and Mrs. Woolf in small passages, for the details are often entertaining, even though their function may be trivial. But I cannot read the neat but simple Mr. Hemingway, nor the inarticulate (though doubtless profound) Mr. Faulkner, and I can see no reason why I should be asked to try. I am a student of literature, not an anthropologist, and I have better ways of spending the few years remaining to me." Yvor Winters, "Problems for the Modern Critic of Literature," *Hudson Review*, autumn, 1956.

lect of the serious novel was accidental rather than willful. I
realized, of course, that a novelist communicates with people by
way of his novels—but only if his novels are read. Wasn't this,
I asked myself, a situation, a crisis, in which some supplementary
form of communication ought to be tried? If a number of serious
novelists could be persuaded to talk about what they thought they
were doing and why they were doing it, I knew very well that
I and everybody else who is concerned with serious fiction would
be interested, and I believed that some of those who are not so
concerned might discover reasons why they ought to be.

To begin with, I put the idea to some novelists that I knew,
and the immediate response was what I had expected. Saul Bellow,
for instance, stated his position in this fashion: "There is only one
way to defeat the enemy, and that is to write as well as one can.
The best argument is an undeniably good book." Later on, Flannery O'Connor remarked that in writing about fiction instead of
writing fiction she felt like a Displaced Person. Ralph Ellison's
essay begins: "Surely it would be of more value for a novelist to
write novels than to spend his energies discussing the novel." Yet
Mr. Bellow and Miss O'Connor and Mr. Ellison did write essays,
and so did the seven others. This was, the ten agreed, a time for
speaking out.

The contributors are all serious and talented novelists, and if
the reader thinks of other novelists from whom he would have
liked to hear, that is evidence in favor of my contention that
serious novelists currently abound. There are considerable differences in age, reputation, productivity, and talent, and in that
respect the book may be called representative, but it was not
planned to represent particular schools or trends. For my purposes
the only important question was whether an individual was a
serious novelist and was likely to have something to say about
the writing of fiction. No topics were assigned or suggested; each
contributor was simply invited to talk about such matters as

seemed urgent to him. Whatever these men and women had to say would, I believed, be worth listening to.

Now the findings are in, and the reader may examine them. Our novelists, it becomes clear, are not altogether happy about their present situation. They are disturbed both by the talk in highbrow circles about the death of the novel and by the middle-brow demands for affirmative fiction useful for propaganda purposes. They have, most of them, financial problems—such problems as are soberly set forth by Harvey Swados and John Brooks. They believe, as Saul Bellow and Jessamyn West point out, that the age places particular difficulties in the way of the novelist.

But not one of them is discouraged, nor is anyone much concerned with his grievances. They all intend to go on writing, and they all expect to be heard. They do not deny that they have problems, but they believe that problems exist to be solved. They believe, moreover, that their serious problems are not those presented by this time and this place but, rather, those that the novelist has always confronted. In their definition and analysis of these perennial problems there is no unanimity; on the contrary, the reader may sometimes get the impression that this contributor and that are engaging in debate, though actually contributors had no opportunity to read one another's essays. But if they disagree on many matters, in fundamentals they stand together.

Their central common quality is their affirmativeness. Wright Morris begins with a broad discussion of the failures of the imagination in America, whereas Mark Harris begins with a personal misadventure, but one arrives as surely as the other at the conclusion that the novel is needed. After his careful examination of the economic problems of the writer, the situation in the publishing business, and the shortcomings of the critics, Harvey Swados records not only his determination to go on writing but also his belief that the future is likely to be better for novelists than the present. Herbert Gold's impatience with novelists of several sorts grows out of his sense, vigorously expressed, of the greatness of which the novel is capable. Paul Darcy Boles defines what he is trying to do in terms of the satisfactions the books of others have given him.

None of the contributors indulges in shop talk, but all of them are passionately concerned with the craft of fiction. For them, however, the craft is a mystery and not a set of rules to be memorized. They are likely to talk, you may notice, about how a writer feels when he is writing rather than about what he does. You see quite clearly in Wright Morris's essay that, for the serious novelist, the writing of fiction is a way of life.

For all of these writers are affirming more than the importance of a literary form. Miss O'Connor, indeed, speaks openly and with feeling about the relation between her writing and her religion. No one else does quite that, but Miss West comes close enough in her tribute to openness and Saul Bellow in his allusions to love. "At its best," Herbert Gold writes, "the art of the novel tells us more than we can find out elsewhere about love and death." Mr. Harris speaks of the novelist's concern with "the excitement of being an adult human being in a world so wondrous with hope and sorrow and loyalty and defeat and anguish and delight." "Not the least of the jobs of the contemporary novelist," says John Brooks, "is that of rescuing American society from the charge that it doesn't exist." "A novelist begins with disorder and disharmony," according to Mr. Bellow, "and he goes toward order by an unknown process of the imagination." "In our time," Ralph Ellison reminds us, "the most articulate art form for defining ourselves and for asserting our humanity is the novel."

All of these men and women believe in the importance of the novel because they believe in the importance of something else— of what Henry James called "felt experience," of awareness, of imagination. Against this belief all theories about the death of the novel shatter themselves. If what was involved were simply the submergence of a literary form, no one would be seriously disturbed. That the writing of epic poetry appears to be impossible in our time occasions little sorrow, for in our time the imagination finds expression in other forms. But there is no substitute now available for the novel, and those who talk about the death of the novel are talking about the death of the imagination.

In this book the reader will find evidence that the novel is not dead and that it is not going to submit docilely to the murder that is plotted against it. Better, stronger evidence will be found in the novels that the contributors and no small number of their contemporaries have written, and the book will serve its principal purpose only if it leads readers, such readers as need to be led, to discover for themselves the present vitality of serious fiction.

GRANVILLE HICKS

Grafton, New York
April 8, 1957

THE LIVING NOVEL

Saul Bellow
Distractions of a Fiction Writer

ON THE one hand literature, tragic as well as comic, belongs in the realm of happiness; on the other hand writers are often unhappy and distracted. They have never been examined so earnestly before. The writer hasn't often in the past been called upon to give an account of himself. When the poet tries to come between Brutus and Cassius during their quarrel they throw him out. They don't ask him to give historical reasons for being a poet. He is too unimportant for that. And I believe his unimportance in that day to have been one of his advantages. Now there are people who devote themselves to the study of poets and who badger and investigate them. Poets and other writers are asked—they ask themselves—many serious and weighty questions. Which means either that society has a larger stake in literature than it used to have, or that it can't resist meddling with anything related to happiness with a view to doing it some damage.

What are some of these questions—or charges or indictments? Let us say that the writer (in this case a novelist) is in the customary solitude of his room, and that he is under a strain and that his writing is not at its best. Today it is hard for him to declare with Joseph Conrad that the world is a temple. He would have to assert, "It *is* a temple." And that would already be a mistake. The feeling of sacredness is beyond price, but the assertion has very little value. Therefore the novelist will make no assertion for the sake of strengthening himself. He will rather ask, "Why didn't you choose a different sort of work, something you could do wholeheartedly every day? Why do you write fiction? You can't build a business on inspirations. Besides, what makes you think it's wanted? Maybe it's an unhistorical and superfluous occupation you've chosen. The whole world is in motion, blazing. And what are you doing? You're doing nothing commensurate. Only sitting here alone, oddly faithful to things you learned as a boy. They taught you the Palmer method in school, so here you are still covering pages with words. You go on about men and women, families and marriages, divorces, crime and flight, murders, weddings, wars, rises and declines, simplicities and complexities, blessedness and agony, and it's all largely imaginary. Who asks you to write such things? What the devil are you doing here? What's all this about dead and non-existent people—Priams and Hecubas? Who is this Hecuba anyway and what are you to her? You're a foolish busybody," says the writer to himself. "Adding book to book. What for? Aren't there enough books? Even King Solomon was already complaining that there was a 'sufficiency' of them. You are practicing a peculiar and, some say, an obsolete art. You may have an inherited Jewish taste for such things."

Such are the questions or doubts or charges. I believe they can be answered. And though it is sad and possibly harmful that they must be heard, it is not necessarily fatal. Eros manages somehow to survive analysis; and somehow imagination survives criticism. In either case the rising of an imperious need abolishes all the questions. "Do you feel it necessary to do this? Then, for the love of God, do it," says the need. If it argues at all.

As a young man Rilke made a pilgrimage to Russia to see Tolstoi. As I have heard the story, he followed the impatient old man around filling his ears with his problems about writing. Tolstoi couldn't bear it. He had exchanged art for religion, and all this seemed very trifling to him. "*Vous voulez écrire?*" he said. "*Eh bien, écrivez donc! Écrivez!*" What else is there to say? Do it if you must, and don't fuss so about it.

Nevertheless, there are certain distractions.

The novelist is distracted; he writes for someone and that someone is sure to be distracted. The Wedding Guest is distracted when the Ancient Mariner stops him. The Mariner lets his two companions go and holds the Guest with his glittering eye. Amid the distractions of merrymaking the Bride is led to the altar, ready to forswear all others. The Guest can only tear his hair as he hears the loud bassoon. He is cut off from his beloved distractions by the power of art and he cannot choose but hear. This is the position we are all in; we resist the spell but we also desire it.

"Why should I end my distractions for you?" That is the question asked of the writer. For there are more things that solicit the attention of the mind than there ever were before. The libraries and museums are full, great storehouses with their thousands of masterpieces in every style. Their vast wealth excites our ambition. It can make a Dr. Faustus out of many an educated man. It menaces him with death by distraction. But everyone on every level is exposed to this danger. The giant producers of goods need our defenseless attention. They catch us on the run and through the eyes and ears fill us with the brand names of cars and cigarettes and soaps. And then news and information distract us. Bad art distracts us. Genuine culture is also, as I've already noted, distracting. Lastly, there are the inner demands of memory, desire, fantasy, anxiety, and the rest. These are perhaps the most tyrannical. The great outer chaos drives us inward, and in our own small kingdoms we indulge our favorite distractions.

The following quotation shows the elementary forms of common distraction. It is taken from a popular booklet, *The Handbook of Beauty*, by Constance Hart. The chapter title is "Double-Duty Beauty Tricks":

"While doing housework: You can keep your face creamed, your hair in pin curls; you can practice good standing and walking posture; when you're sitting at the kitchen counter peeling potatoes you can do your ankle exercises, and foot strengtheners, and also practice good sitting posture. . . . While telephoning (at home, of course) you can do neck exercises; brush your hair, do ankle exercises, eye exercises, foot strengtheners and chin and neck exercises; practice good standing or sitting posture; even massage your gums (while listening to the other person). . . . While reading or watching TV: You can brush your hair, massage your gums; do your ankle and hand exercises and foot strengtheners; do some back and bust exercises; massage your scalp, use the abrasive treatment for removing superfluous hair."

Here we see basic distraction. Here even personal beauty is put on the Taylor system of industrial efficiency. All this simultaneous writhing and plucking suggests both Willow Run and the torments of Hell. Such grim energy can only be drawn from the feeling that life's shortness requires us to combine our activities, combine and combine, and multiply the levels of consciousness and of muscular coordination layer upon layer, on a sandwich principle. We are not perfect. We must perfect ourselves, we must exhaust ourselves. Maybe, too, there is a perverse desire for freedom in this. Dominated by no single activity, we are free; free but not tranquil; at leisure but not idle, since all the while

4

we strive for perfection. No, the face, the neck, the bust, the skin, the mind are not good as they are, and we must tirelessly improve them. By so doing we deny the power of death over us because as long as we're getting better there's no reason why we should die. But I think the ruling principle behind all of this can be stated as follows: Don't give yourself wholly to any single thing. Divide and multiply.

What a fate to marry a woman who follows such instructions! But what shall we say about the fate of the author whose novel she holds in her hand?—if she has a hand to spare. How is he to get her attention? Can he hold her with his glittering eye? Why, he himself suffers from such diseases. He, like everyone else, is subject to vanity, not willingly. He also is deafened by the noise of life, by cries and claims and counterclaims and fantasy and desire and ambition for perfection, by false hope and error and the fear of death.

But distraction is not necessarily inimical to the imagination. Novels are floated upon distraction. They begin in the midst of it. On the first page of *Anna Karenina* we are told, "All was confusion in the house of the Oblonskys." Distraction is one of the subjects of Tolstoi's masterpiece. Society is in Tolstoi's view a system of distractions. Anna and Vronsky are drawn apart by its disapproval of their union. Vronsky grows bored; he has no proper work or center of attention, for love, or the purest sort of attention to another, can't be sustained day by day. Love is not an occupation. Therefore Vronsky falls away. Anna's brother Oblonsky makes a last attempt to obtain his brother-in-law Karenin's consent to a divorce. Anna's life depends on this.

"After an excellent dinner with unlimited cognac . . . Oblonsky arrived at the Countess Lydia Ivanovna's," says Tolstoi. In the course of the evening Oblonsky falls asleep, and when he awakes he steals out of the house, forgetting the appeal he was to have made to Karenin. Next morning he receives Karenin's final refusal.

I don't see how we can avoid blaming Oblonsky for his sister's suicide. A normally decent man, no worse than most, hearty, a good liver, he loves his sister, yes, but he is unable to keep his attention fixed upon her need. He is not a monster of selfishness; he is distracted. The attention is supplied by Tolstoi in the writing of the novel. His method is one of deliberate slowness and simplification, a contemplative slowness which brings order and unity out of confusion. We never go from distraction to attention (of a certain sort) without experiencing a triumphant emotion. Distractions give force to a work of art by their resolution, and the novelist works more deeply with distractions than any other kind of artist. Many events fall upon us, assail us with claims on our time and our judgment; waves of disintegrative details wash over us and threaten to wear away all sense of order and proportion. The novelist begins at a great depth of distraction and difficulty. Sometimes, as in James Joyce's *Ulysses*, he risks total immersion in distraction. I don't say that the novelist knows what order is; but he relies upon his imagination to lead him toward it. In a work of art the imagination is the sole source of order. There are critics who assume that you must begin with order if you are to end with it. Not so. A novelist begins with disorder and disharmony, and he goes toward order by an unknown process of the imagination. And anyway, the order he achieves is not the order that ideas have. Critics need to be reminded of this, I think. Art is the speech of artists. The rules are not the same as those in Science or Philosophy. No one knows what the power of the imagination comes from or how much distraction it can cope with. We are now told that it has reached its limit. The distraction is supposed to be too broad for love and too deep for beauty and too agonizing for any order. And so we are told by critics that the novel is dead. These people can't know what the imagination is nor what its powers are. I wish I could believe in their good-natured objectivity. But I can't. I should like to disregard them, but that is a little difficult because they have a great deal of power. Not real power, perhaps, but power of a sort. And they can be very distracting.

But the deadly earnestness with which they lower the boom! On what? after all. On flowers. On mere flowers.

It occurs to a man that he is a writer. He doesn't obtain a certificate, like a doctor, or take a bar examination, like a lawyer; nor does he apprentice himself, like a tool-and-die maker, or get into a union, like a bricklayer. A novel is written by a man who thinks of himself as a novelist. Unless he makes such an assumption about himself he simply can't do it. The thing is impossible. He has to encounter the world in a particular way. He goes within a sort of tissue which floats about the mind when he is well or collapses upon it when he isn't. It's hard to say exactly where this tissue comes from or what it is, but it is a sign of his autonomy. He has called himself out and anointed himself. No prophet picked him. And so he has neither supernatural nor social assistance. Now, aren't we Americans fond of self-made men? Of some of them, yes. And to this peculiar self-election of the man who goes about calling himself a novelist there is no visible barrier, at least. Well, then, let's say that the anointee is carried away by the force of his imagination; he gives utterance to the images it brings him, and with a certain arrogance he assumes that what he writes needs to be read and will be read. The origin of this arrogance, if arrogance is what it is, is rather mysterious too. In fact, from any sensible, rational point of view the whole thing is bewildering. Still, as it begins privately and harms no one there are no objections. None will be heard as long as the interests of power are not touched.

Society doesn't do much to encourage this self-elected man; on the contrary it subjects him to many negative pressures. Is it angry with the imagination? Does it perhaps hate it? That may

7

well be. At any rate it holds the imagination under suspicion. For there are always leading activities which society needs and sponsors. Sometimes it is the lawgiver who is in the highest place, and sometimes the priest, and sometimes the general. With us it is the businessman, the administrator, the political leader, the military man. These have the power; they are the representative men; in them manhood is mirrored. They honor themselves and are universally honored and imitated as the possessors of power and virtue. They rule armies and industries and publishing empires and build atomic reactors and legislate for us all. A modern writer, when he comes to speak of their powers, is forced to speak vaguely because he doesn't really know what they're doing. Any connection between art and authority has for some time been broken. Who now is Cromwell's secretary? Was it Mr. Stephen Early? Is it Mr. Hagerty? Well, then, if it is true that the writer has no actual connection with power, and that he is separated from the main current of things not only by the lack of certain dignities but also because he is compelled by his self-authorization to live in a manner different from most other men, why doesn't he by the daring of his imagination alone make a leap into the councils of State or into the Pentagon or a Cabinet meeting? Oddly enough, he doesn't even expect it of himself. He accepts timidly all the restrictions of the rule of experience. The demons of firsthand knowledge, documentation and naturalistic accuracy, have seized him. *The Red Badge of Courage* was probably the last American novel to be taken wholly from the imagination, and there are indignant letters in the old *Dial* by Civil War veterans denouncing Crane for the technical errors which, not then experienced in war, he had made. We are a nation devoted to facts, and we don't like to waste time with books that give the wrong dope about shipwrecks on the coast of Bohemia. We like to get things straight. Otherwise we feel that we are wasting valuable time. And if a man writes a book we think we are justi-

fied in asking him, as though we were about to hire him, about
his qualifications and his experience. For we really feel that experience is intrinsically valuable and we have the same acquisitive
attitude toward it as toward other things of value. Experience
can never be bad, we seem to believe; the more one has had, the
better. While this attitude may be justified in some respects, I
think it ought to be pointed out that the disorder of experience
is distraction. Imagination may do with experience or with non-
experience precisely what it likes. By refusing to write about
anything with which he is not thoroughly familiar, the American
writer confesses the powerlessness of the imagination and accepts
its relegation to an inferior place.

"All the qualities of a man acquire dignity when he knows
that the service of the collectivity that owns him needs them,"
wrote William James in his essay "The Moral Equivalent of War."
Well, the writer certainly must think that if the collectivity knew
what its best interests were it would see that it needed him as
much as it does—let's not go so far as to say the Secretaries of
State or Defense—but as much as it needs psychiatrists, who deal
also with the confusions of experience, or television directors.
But since the writer of novels has found the oil and anointed himself he need not deceive himself about the "collectivity." He can't
feel that it needs him. Not unless he creates a sensation or makes
a great fortune. For of course money will turn the trick. "If,"
continues William James, "If proud of the collectivity, his own
pride rises in proportion." There doesn't seem to be much of this
pride around. In modern times the feelings and thoughts of writers
have gone counter to the general direction. If they have gone
with the collectivity—the mass—it has been on the terms of the
mass and not their own.

American writers have often described themselves as loafers,
vagabonds, beggars and bums. Thoreau sits apart from the economy in idleness beside Walden Pond. Walt Whitman describes

himself as one of the "roughs." Vachel Lindsay wrote *A Handy Guide for Beggars* out of his experience as a preacher of his Gospel of Beauty. Writers have stood aside from the ordinary duties of their fellow citizens. I don't perhaps so much mean duties as I mean the routines of the milltowns, the mining towns, and the great cities. Others get up in the morning and ride in crowds to their work. Not the self-anointed writer. He sits up in his room, writing, a freer man. Or is he freer? Is he free? Perhaps he feels a weak and treasonable fear in his soul at doing something so hard to explain to the others, the early-morning passengers on the Milwaukee Avenue street car.

"I loafe and invite my soul," says Walt Whitman.

Well, perhaps his counterpart today does, too. Perhaps. I hope so, because his imagination requires the tranquil attitude. But chances are that he is working, bitterly working, in an effort to meet his brothers of the office and factory sympathetically. The odds are good that he is literally a brother and comes out of the same mass. And now for some strange reason he is trying to throw a bridge from this same place, from a room in Chicago to, let us say, Ahab, to Cervantes, to Shakespeare, to the Kings of the old Chronicles, to Genesis. For he says, "Aren't we still part of the same humanity, children of Adam?" So he invites his soul away from distractions.

But sometimes he can feel in the very streets that the energies of the population have been withdrawn to mass activity, industry, and money. At midday in an American city you are aware of a certain emptiness about the houses. You hear the organ groaning in dissolution as the scenes of the soap opera change in the kitchen below, beneath the table where you sit writing. And sometimes the suspicion arises that maybe the Studebaker, maybe the Bendix have absorbed man's highest powers. Can the intellectual, esthetic, moral genius of the human race have come to a stop? That's impossible. Aeronautical engineers have just shown that the globe can be circumnavigated in a forty-five-hour nonstop flight. That is genius—to lift man and metal from the ground and send them around the face of the earth. Before such an achievement nobody ought to be bored and no one ought to feel isolated. The shuddering of the organ, the vacant dullness of a world that is (temporarily) not a temple have no great importance. The smell of beer on the dark stairs is nothing. The absence of a human contact is merely temporary. The page in the typewriter describing a certain conversation that never actually took place is an offering placed on the altar of certain gods who—who aren't around just now. But they'll be back, for in time everyone will miss them. Remember Thoreau sitting beside his pond. The industry of his neighbors failed to break his connection with nature. "You are," the writer may tell himself, "joined to your fellows in a better way. For in actual fact how well are they joined to one another? They form a very loose, friable mass. The comradeship of the assembly line isn't very thick; nor that of the bowling alley, community club, tavern, package store. Camps and barracks were different. But there you drew sneers and hatred if you read books or spoke in your own style. Remember your loyalty to the human spirit, and don't drag after the mob protesting that you're not a writer at all but a fisherman or farmer. It would be fear only that made you say such things; the shame of being divorced by difference from other men, and also the fear of the savage strength of the many."

Thus the fiction writer may talk to himself—when he's distracted. For when he is actually at work the excitement of the imagination carries him and he needs no justification as a vagabond or dedicated idler who by his example will recall his money-chasing brethren to sit down with him and feel their hearts and tell sad tales, and be tranquil before the beauty of the external world, and all the rest of it. No, then he is too busy.

But once in a while, he is visited by the thought that he is sitting still in the midst of the most widespread destruction. Man's hatred of himself has led in this century to the wildest of wars and demolition of the human image in camps and jails built for that purpose. Bodies stacked like firewood we have seen; and the bodies of the massacred exhumed for the gold in their teeth we have seen too. And even the so-called years of peace have been years of war. The buying and consumption of goods that keep the economy going the writer sitting in his room may envision as acts of duty, of service, of war. By our luxury we fight, too, eating and drinking and squandering to save our form of government, which survives because it produces and sells vast quantities of things. This sort of duty or service, he thinks, may well destroy our souls. They are taken from us and put to strange uses. Under it all perhaps, he reflects, is a hatred of individual being. "Let it be obliterated," is the secret message that we hear. And many in their hearts answer, "Yea, so be it." It may be that this is the hidden purpose of the frantic distraction to which we are exposed. If that is the case, the writer, like the minister of a religion, feels that perhaps he is anachronistic.

"The priest departs, the divine literatus comes," said Walt Whitman. He felt that the office of the poet absorbed the sacerdotal one. In *Democratic Vistas* he gave the poet the responsibility of creating a type of man, an archetype he called it, and he offered himself as a model or representative. We have to begin somewhere. Touch me, he said, and you touch a man. I am not different from others; they are not different from me. What I assume you shall assume. This is not always understood for the act of love that it was. Between the radically unlike there is no love. So the creation of an archetype was to belong to the poet—and the humanist, the scholar. Well, now, where are these people? You can see them around the country in various places, most commonly in colleges and universities. They are different, though many of them try not to be. They are powerless. The universities are the warehouses of culture. Let us imagine a man who lives in Akron, Ohio, and teaches the history of the Italian Renaissance. It is dreadful to think what he has to reconcile. Or he teaches ethics, and takes part in departmental politics. He behaves shabbily and his own heart cannot bear the contrast. What I am trying to say is that certain ideas can't be held idly. Attempted containment of them is ruin. Lying in his bed in his impoverished attic, Raskolnikov is ashamed of the thoughts of mastery that come into his head; this shame, like a radioactive material, eats through the wall of moral restraint, and issues destructively. He commits a double murder. But it is not only ideas of evil that become destructive. Ideas of good, held in earnest, may be equally damaging to the passive thinker. His passivity puts him in self-contempt. This same contempt may estrange him from the ideas of good. He lives below them and feels dwarfed. On certain occasions a hero in thought, he has become abject in fact, and he cannot be blamed for feeling that he is not doing a man's work. He reads about man's work in the paper. Men are planning new bond issues, molding public opinion, solving the crisis of the Suez Canal. Men are active. Ideas are passive. Ideas are held in contempt. Literature in these circumstances is contemptible. Of course, it is pleasant to have some poets around. All great empires have had them. We are a great empire and need some too. And so Herod sits in his vast palace of advertising and publicity, and once in a while he hears the voice of John from the dungeon. He doesn't even bother to cut off his head.

The writer has no connection with power, and yet he keeps thinking about it. I offer a few eighteenth and nineteenth century declarations in evidence: "Poets are the unacknowledged legislators of the world." "Give me the making of the songs of a nation, and I care not who makes its laws." "Above all previous lands, a great original literature is surely to become the justification and reliance, (in some respects the sole reliance,) of American democracy."

But I should like to point out that impotence has received more attention from modern writers than any other subject. I use the word "impotence" rather loosely to include the loss or defect of the sympathetic power, the failure of feeling (what Elizabeth Bowen has called "the death of the heart"), as well as literal incapacity. Here is a brief list:

Oblomov: he spends his life in bed.

Moreau in Flaubert's *The Sentimental Education*: a life spent on trifles, utterly spoiled.

Captain Ahab: "I have lost the low enjoying power." He means that he is distracted. Natural beauty is recognized by his mind but it doesn't move him.

Clym Yeobright in *The Return of the Native*: empty of the feeling which Eustacia desires.

The hero of Henry James's "The Beast in the Jungle": empty of feeling.

Dostoevski's hero or anti-hero in *Notes from Underground*: his spite, his coldness, his venom, combined with the greatness of his mind, give him an exceptional stature.

Leopold Bloom: the distracted and impotent man.

I could add hundreds more to this list, from Lawrence or Proust or Hemingway and their innumerable imitators. They all tell the same story. The dread is great, the soul is small; man might be godlike but he is wretched; the heart should be open but it is sealed by fear. If man wretched by nature is represented, what we have here is only accurate reporting. But if it is man in the image of God, man a little lower than the angels who is impotent, the case is not the same. And it is the second assumption, the subangelic one, that writers generally make. For they are prone, as Nietzsche said in *Human, All Too Human*, to exaggerate the value of human personality. I don't know whether exaggeration is quite the word, but what it suggests we can certainly agree with. Why should wretched man need power or wish to inflate himself with imaginary glory? If this is what power signifies it can only be vanity to suffer from impotence. On the nobler assumption he should have at least sufficient power to overcome ignominy and to complete his own life. His suffering, feebleness, servitude then have a meaning. This is what writers have taken to be the justification of power. It should reveal the greatness of man. And if no other power will do this, the power of the imagination will take the task upon itself.

"That undisturbed, innocent, somnambulatory production by which alone anything great can thrive, is no longer possible. Our talents lie before the public. Daily criticism in fifty different places, and gossip caused by them, prevent the appearance of any sound production. He who does not keep aloof from all this and isolate himself by main force, is lost." (Goethe: *Conversations with Eckermann*)

So, if the writer is wise, he will avoid certain books and papers and magazines and social circles. But perhaps wisdom won't help. Everybody talks. The cat is already out of the bag. You go to a party and a psychiatrist tells you that *his* analyst believes literature is dying. This is an act of aggression. But how can a novelist be expected to stay away from parties? He must go, and he must inevitably hear the worst, exposing his somnambulatory innocence to grave dangers. Once more the boom is lowered on the flowers. But they will grow again. There is man's own greatness, and then there is the greatness of his imbecility—both are eternal.

It's only natural that writers should have their enemies. It's the rule of life, among writers as among snakes, mice, and lice. The subtler creatures have subtler enemies. The subtlest of enemies are those who get you over to their own side. You read the authoritative words of an eminent critic; they sound reasonable; you half agree, and then you are distracted and stiflingly depressed.

Finished! We have heard this from Valéry and from T. S. Eliot, from Ortega and from Oswald Spengler, and most recently from the summit of Morningside Heights. We are supposed to be done for. The great dinosaurs are gone; only vestigial Gila monsters remain. Oh, to have once more the unimportance of that poor poet whom Brutus and Cassius threw out! For every poet now there are a hundred custodians and doctors of literature, and dozens of undertakers measuring away at coffins. If only, says D. H. Lawrence in a poem, man were as much man as the lizard is lizard! If only the novelist, though merely a degenerate Gila monster, were at least a true Gila monster! He would sit in the sun, undistracted, and catch flies.

The novelist has been trained to take words seriously, and he thinks he is hearing words of high seriousness. He believes it is the voice of high seriousness saying, "Obsolete. Finished." But what if it were to prove to be the voice of low seriousness instead?

Scholars and critics are often curiously like property owners. They have their lots surveyed. Here the property begins and there it ends. A conservative instinct in them, which every lover of order will recognize and respect, resists extension, calls for limits. And why not? Besides, it's awfully fine to be an epigone. It tickles one so in the self-esteem. But how odd it is that these words "obsolete" and "finished" should never be spoken with regret or pain. The accent is rather one of satisfaction. And this is all the more strange because if the critics are wrong their opinions will do harm. They are certain to be destructive.

The students of literature line up with the epigones. "Thank God!" they say, "it's over. Now we have a field. We can study." Well, it does seem logical that the thing should have an end. The libraries and the secondhand bookstores are very full, as I've al-

ready observed. Isn't it enough that the physical universe over-
whelms us with its immensities? Must the works of man flood us as
well? But I wonder whether novels can be studied with much profit
or even read if we don't continue to write them. Not professional
study but imagination keeps imagination alive. Samuel Butler in
his *Note-books* offers a theory to which I subscribe. ". . . all
things which come to much," he says, "whether they be books,
buildings, pictures or living beings, are suggested by others of
their kind." I wonder what historical reasons there are for this
process of suggestion to stop. And what will happen to *Anna
Karenina* or to the *Iliad* if they are never read by those to whom
they may suggest others of their kind? Literature, all of it, will
then be extinct.

"The novel has died a victim to the loss of an agreed picture
of the Universe, which has faded with the stifling of Christianity
by non-dogmatic idealism and crude materialism." Thus writes
Mr. J. M. Cohen in his recent *History of Western European
Literature*. His is the bluntest, flattest, most Spartan statement of
the position, and I like it because there is something wonderfully
bureaucratic about it. The "agreed picture of the Universe"
appeals especially to me. I like the stoutness of it. It reminds
me of the textbooks I studied in college. "The Crusades were
begun because . . ." "The following developments made possible
the beginning of the Renaissance in Italy . . ." It is always like
that, blunt, plain, and positive. Textbooks told us what the pre-
requisites were for a flourishing literature. The end of feudalism,
the rise of the burghers, the Reformation, the Age of Reason,
the growth of science (et cetera) made possible the great century
of the novel. The method has worked so well (obviously) in
explaining the past that now scholars have decided to project it
into the future. This is a new branch of the historians' art—
made history.

Ever since M. Jourdain, the bourgeois gentleman, discovered

that his everyday speech was Prose, writers have written Literature, painters have painted Art, musicians have composed Music, and now culture-historians create Culture epoch by epoch—past, present, and future.

An agreed picture of the Universe? What is that? And when we have come to know what it means (if we can), must we believe that novels have become poor because they lack it? It has recently been well argued by J. Bronowski in the *Nation* that the imagination of the scientist is not vastly different from that of the artist. Does the scientific imagination also have need of an agreed picture of the Universe? Science quickly changes the agreed pictures. And why does it survive so well the stifling of Christianity?

"Probably all of us, to some extent, share in the misconception of modern literature that dominates illiterate minds," wrote my late friend Isaac Rosenfeld, "that it is divisive and fragmented, reflecting the breakdown of the social order, the decay of capitalism and bourgeois civilization. . . . Such minds, not necessarily of low intelligence, and often brilliant on ground far removed from the arts, betray a fear of modernity; they recoil from experience before it has deeply touched them and never receive more than the disintegrative impression. . . . Yet our age is perhaps the most highly systematizing one in history. . . . The mind that flees disorder is frightened by a multiplicity of choice even more than by chaos; in fact this is its basic image of chaos. . . . it forces a reductive and equalizing system on experience."

The argument that the novel is dying or dead is made by men who shut the door on multiplicity and distraction. They suppose the distraction to be too great for the imagination to overcome. When they speak of an agreed picture what they mean is that we are a mass civilization, doomed to be shallow and centerless. Question: "And what if the soul doesn't accept?" Answer: "It had better. Its acceptance is historically determined." But this smells of bars and prisons. And we started out to talk of literature and happiness! How busy the grimmer impulses are!

Why were we born? What are we doing here? Where are we going? In its eternal naïveté the imagination keeps coming back to these things. It does this when we have an agreed picture and when we haven't. For it isn't an agreed picture that makes man interesting to himself. It isn't history and it isn't culture; the interest is intrinsic. And it's not unfair to ask those literary people who argue that the novel is dead whether their own feelings are fresh or tired. Life quickly wears us out; there is good reason to be tired. But this is not a matter for the tired to settle.

But we are living in what they call an eschatological age. Whole worlds have become as light as ping-pong balls. At lunch we talk about good and evil, death and immortality, and over cocktails metaphysical questions are raised as if the world, like the bottles, might be emptied by dinnertime. Then why should so minor a thing as The Novel escape its moment of question?

A lot of things have been called obsolete. I brooded over Spengler in college. As a Jew I was, in his vocabulary, a Magian and therefore obsolete. Toynbee, unless I am mistaken, has a similar view of Jews, that they are a sort of fossil. Marx and Engels, too, were prophets of obsolescence. For Stalin the kulaks were obsolete; for Hitler, all the "inferior" breeds of men. In the dustbins of various reform movements are found numerous orthodoxies called obsolete. And we all know—what else does Mr. Cohen mean when he speaks of the stifling of Christianity?—that God has been called obsolete. I don't mean to say that there is no such thing as obsolescence. I merely wish to show that the term "obsolete," derived from evolutionary thought, has a place of some importance in the history of modern persecution. Far, far down in the scale of power, far from Rome and Berlin and Leningrad, in certain academic and critical circles we hear it said that a particular kind of imagination is now obsolete. The objective conditions necessary for its existence are supposedly gone. I've never heard it stated in the same circles that money is obsolete or that social advancement and distinction are obsolete. Apparently these things are hardier and don't require the same agreement as to the nature of the Universe.

Well, such an issue can never be settled in debate. Neither the denials of academic people nor the affirmations of writers can make much difference. "To believe in the existence of human beings as such is love," says Simone Weil. This is what makes the difference. It is possible—all too possible—to say when we have read one more modern novel: "So what? What do I care? You yourself, the writer, didn't really care." It is all too often like that. But this caring or believing or love alone matters. All the rest, obsolescence, historical views, manners, agreed views of the Universe, is simply nonsense and trash. If we don't care, don't immediately care, then perish books both old and new, and novelists, and governments, too! If we do care, if we believe in the existence of others, then what we write is necessary.

The writer asks himself, "Why shall I write this next thing?" It is still possible, despite all theories to the contrary, to answer, "Because it *is necessary*." A book, any book, may easily be superfluous. But to manifest love—can that be superfluous? Is there so much of it about us? Not so much. It is still rare, still wonderful. It is still effective against distraction.

Paul Darcy Boles
The Vision Then and Now

SOMETIMES, for a novelist, the stars look very cold about the sky. Then again, something warm and quick happens inside him and the world loosens up; words spring as easily as muscles when a man walks; and the stars are places that are not cold, not aloof, but pleasantly normal and full of awesomeness.

For a long time, when I was a child, wanting to be a novelist from the age of seven, everything that was printed seemed to contain its own breed of magic. It became special just because it was printed. There were, as with a child, no second thoughts and no first critical thoughts. There was a mélange of hearty fare: *Tom Swift* and *Les Misérables*, all in the same gulp; there were *Moby Dick* and *Kazan* and *Baree, Son of Kazan*. All at once there were the novels, then like a rich green world, of Louisa May Alcott. Everything that later seemed prissy and stilted and carefully moralistic was no stumbling block at all: the eye glided over things like that as a fish glides, for the pure joy of being alive in water. The Gary Public Library was a warm expanse with adventure flickering from every shelf; the dark nose-filling smell of old books, old bindings, seemed to reach out with welcome. It seemed to me then that the world was beautifully ordered for reading: dimly, I wondered why more people did not make libraries their headquarters. Snow looked better from a library's windows: when seen above the rim of a book (oh, Doctor Dolittle: oh, your post office, and oh, Polynesia, your parrot!) it seemed to drift down and fill the sills with a rosily cheerful quality, something that partook of the book and the image of the book in the mind. And the shuffling of adults in the distance was nothing but a signal that people were alive in the world which was an extension of, and part of, and indistinguishable from, books. In the long gray dusk when it was time and past time to go home I would still be reading as I went down the library steps and stood teetering on the curb: the great white whale would be out there somewhere in front of me—not far; just as close as the vegetable truck turning the corner and spattering grains of slush over my galoshes. To a child this time of complete faith in all books seems forever. It has no bounds; it feels infinite, stretching ahead of him the way one summer can be made of millions of years.

This vision of the full life, of mankind as part of books and the novel as part of man's life, began burning early and it has never really gone out. I can still go back and recapture the enormous feeling of discovery which came with the first knowledge of reading: I can remember the book (in fact, I still have it somewhere, and a very slight aura of magic still stays around it, though it is dull reading) which would be mine, with my name written carefully on the flyleaf, as soon as I could read it aloud. Its title was *Father Thrift and His Animal Friends*. I was five, then, and it is not the story so much as the sensation of giant doors opening which sight of the dark green cover and the bright illustrations brings back now, like the smell of certain perfume evoking the thought of a lovely girl you once knew.

I was lucky in that, at home, few restrictions were placed on what I read. I remember that one summer night, my grandmother, inspired by some editorial in an educational journal (I have a notion it was the old *Literary Digest*) put a clamp on the works of Mr. Edgar Rice Burroughs: No more Tarzan, she said; and, like the Boston public during the bans of Watch and Ward, my curiosity was instantly inflamed and not to be assuaged. Using an Eveready flashlight as reading lamp, I explored Pellucidar and romped with the golden lion all night long: in the morning I reflected that it hadn't truly been worth it, and that Kipling, who wasn't banned, really gave you more for your money. These first flickerings of discrimination came and went and came back again; for some reason, inexplicable, some books were better than other books, just as some teachers were better than other teachers, some experiences, not always outwardly more attractive, more lasting and memorable than others.

I think I was lucky too because, at that time, children's reading was not viewed with quite the owlish and efficient solemnity it is now: I cannot recall being forced into the narrow valley of works labeled *Children 6 to 9*, or *Ages 10-12*. I was a hound loose in a world of rich scents and magnificently interlaced trails; if after a hard hunt I brought home nothing but a rabbit, it made no difference; there was God's plenty to seek and find, and chances were good that next day I would pick up the reek of a mountain lion. I was also like the pioneer scout free in the limitless forests and grasses of early America, with the same voraciousness, casual waste, and minute-by-minute exaltation at the unrolling of experience, the same impatience with anything that smelled of rules.

That was the boy's vision; and it has not changed too much

today. That is, the early impetus was strong enough so that the feeling is still there; I cannot go into any library, private or public, without a sensation of immense revelations about to be made. I cannot sit down in front of a thousand sheets of paper to begin writing a novel without the same excited, tremendous feeling: an emotion that is like stout Cortez's men, staring at each other with a wild surmise. All the potential gold of the earth seems to be about to reveal itself to me; all the massive secrets of mankind, the unspoken secrets, seem about to speak. The finished work never satisfies me; an hour after I have written the last word of a novel I feel a tapering off of that splendid high mood of discovery which aimed so far and expected so infinitely much and, it seems to me, came up with so little. All the same, in a week, or two weeks, and at most a month, the feeling comes back —it is indescribably strong, and in some ways it is like an explorer who, after spending a little time in civilization, suddenly, over his drink on the cool veranda, remembers the green sweet hot pulse of the jungle, and knows he has to go in there again.

I don't think any novelist ever thinks he has said it all and can stop. I think this is especially true of American novelists. I know that my own lack of patience is not so much an unwillingness to realize the need for a few great rules as it is furious inward chafing at the bit, a central need for the expression of place and mood and time, and I believe this is inherent in the American novel. It is something that stands back of everything written by Mark Twain, for instance. It tells me that our life in this place can't be pinned down, but can only be lived and, in the novel, interpreted by illumination on paper. It is seldom recollected in tranquillity, because it is here with me, here and now, always happening. Its colors and shapes and sizes aren't like anything else. They are not like the forest of Arden or the fountains of Versailles or the wind bending the reeds down the Nile. They are quicker, bigger, tougher, more terrible, less static. The light is different than it is anywhere else, and the people are different; there is no one thing you can call them; they can't be tabbed and pigeonholed. Our speech itself changes from one day to the next: the land changes overnight: not even the mountains are constant. Love blazes, hate is incandescent, humor is funnier. A novelist can use the words of Shakespeare, Marlowe, Jonson, Webster—Tom Wolfe used them, Herman Melville used them— or he can clip language to a new speech with its own rhythms and inner meanings—Crane tried it, Hemingway did it—or he can curse at the stupidity of indirection and try to summon a direction from surrealism—Henry Miller, Kenneth Patchen— and he will still die knowing he has not said it all. He will know ten thousand things remain to be said.

Yet I have always felt that the novelist in America often works out of more tradition than he recognizes. It is a very old tradition and in no way local. It haunts me every day to know, deep in the bone, that the builders and sculptors and musicians and painters and storytellers of medieval Europe, working out of faith alone, faith in the Hand of Power, somehow—who knows in what amazing ways?—sent that power into America. We cannot deny our tradition; fiercely as we wish to be ourselves, with no "decadent" influences, anything lasting that any man or woman ever wrote in the world is part of us. We cannot deny our tradition; but we can build past the old tradition with a tradition of our own, in our lives, that becomes an essential part of the whole history of the novel.

I think this is being done. I don't think it complacently; a novelist has very little real time to assess the work of other novelists. And even if he has, he is likely to murmur to himself, *Good Job*, or *Fine*, or, *My God, if that sold fifty thousand copies I should've been a stonemason!* He may be willing, each morning of his life, to stand at the grave of Chaucer bearing green boughs, but he is wary about exposing himself as a champion of any particular form or school or type of writing; he has himself to look out for. His armor fits naturally and he keeps it on solidly, except when he is writing. He doesn't want to praise because he is, many times, a bundle of carefully concealed superstitions, and he feels that to praise may be to lose some integral part of himself, to throw away just the extra force and strength out of which he writes. Anyhow, he has seen what happens to the advocates of certain ways, particular methods, of writing; he has seen writers, novelists whom he respected, make asses of themselves at conferences and in symposiums. He doesn't really believe that genuine writing can be taught, or even guided very far. He knows that the days of the Mermaid Tavern are drowned in history; and for that matter, what did Shakespeare have to learn from Ben Jonson? To write in Latin? He—this twentieth century United States novelist—is inclined to believe what novelists themselves have said; Fitzgerald's letters to his daughter; Joseph Conrad's credos; the criticism and the letters of D. H. Lawrence. He believes, there, with responses that come from the marrow. He believes that when John Donne speaks:

> At the round Earth's imagin'd corners, blow
> Your trumpets, Angels, and arise, arise . . .

it is infinitely more important than the voice of the critic which stifles the voice of the poet in T. S. Eliot, when Mr. Eliot sets about proving that John Donne was not such a much of a poet after all.

Perhaps novelists should praise their own kind more often; should make more of their contemporaries. I don't think it will be done. In spirit I am against it; the living minute is the time for work, and silent approval is sometimes enough. I am sure that novelists know more, are more aware, than most of the baby critics give them credit for. They know instinctively, automatically. They can receive any number of intellectual insults

from such flatulent puffers as *Time* and *Life,* and know these are
not worth answering; that the only anger worth expending is
against death-in-life, and that to answer death-in-life with the
affirmation of a real novel is their first job. They know—at least
many do—that the second they become involved in literary controversy it is bad for them; a waste of time and spirit. They learn
to control wild anger at ignorant people, and simply to hate the
ignorance itself.

All this is hard learning; so I do not blame novelists for protecting themselves against the assault which is a flood—a flood
of enemies—once the gates are down. When a novelist is setting
out, for the first time, with the life even shorter and the craft
even longer to learn than Chaucer's words have said, he is defiant,
all right, but he is also naked. He is open to the snubs of the
cheapest speed-reviewer who ever rattled out a paragraph. He
has, if he is any good, given all there was in him to give in that
first novel; yet, also if he is any good, he realizes the shadowy
presence of deep resources still untapped. He knows he has many,
many more things to say, perhaps in half a hundred different
ways, before he dies. He feels the critic, or the speed-reviewer, as
part of that amorphous body of possible enemies waiting to damn
him. He equates them, in a dark lump, with radio, television,
advertising—anything glib and unfelt—and he is coiled like a
spring to hit back. He may come out of this invisible but potent
confusion, and he may not. If he is naturally strong enough,
and naturally affiliated with his sources, and, by all means, naturally able to laugh at himself, chances are he will escape. What
he has escaped is another enemy, in himself. What he has escaped
is the inability ever to slip out of his armor and write as he
knows he can.

And he is conscious of this escape; will be conscious of it
throughout his writing life.

I think we have lost good work because of this devil of enemy-consciousness; I also think we have gained good work because of it. What we have lost, even though it is recaptured in bits once in a while, is the clean and well sunned feeling that was alive in Europe up to the First World War, and that came to its highest flowering after that war, in Paris, Rome, Vienna: the feeling that all writers were creatures who set out, on a sacred, not-to-be-disturbed path, to change the look of the world. It was the culmination of the European gift of dignity to the writer, particularly the poet and the novelist, in his chosen profession. It was the sort of feeling that works into the pores and that generates, not suspicion, not teacup controversy, but great lively openhearted brawls, and much good prose and poetry. It was a hybrid flowering, true: an essentially genial blossom grown on the old and already bitter-rooted stalk of European dissension and fear. But the blossom itself was what mattered. Everything was new, everything had the guts to shine; for all the dadaists and imagists and congenial drunks with no talent but a lot of talk, there was a spirit walking through American letters. I was too young then to be writing anything more serious than a blood-and-chill serial, read aloud each day to the other members of the sixth-grade English class, but I was affected. I was affected later, and became an affirmer. I knew, suddenly, some time back there in the late 1920's or the early thirties, not simply that I would be a novelist: but in general, and in outlines so broad I can still only sketch them, what kind of novelist I would be. The outlines were broad but fiery. I can still see them.

Then we lost all that; I wouldn't know where it went. I have a suspicion that it was cast out as part of our depression emotions, looked on as flippantly sinful; so that with the flapper's old frock the American ashcan received—temporarily, for we are not all that stupid—the works of Fitzgerald, Ezra Pound, Hergesheimer, and others. Another spirit, bleak and ominous but strangely cleansing, walked through our land. This time it didn't have much obvious connection with Europe. It smelled somewhat like canned heat on the breaths of the—literally—starving bums along North Clark, in Chicago. It looked like the slight, ashy cloud of cinders and dust swirling in the wake of a rattler, swarming with hunched migrant workers, bound for God knows where, "someplace where there's still money, bud!" It sounded like the echoes in the Carlsbad caves; the voice came rich with dry but solid reassurance, from the White House: the echoes went on ringing flatter and flatter until they died. What novelists gained, even when they didn't know they were gaining it, was the ability to look long and critically at themselves, and at all the people around them. The genial blossom on the European stalk that might under better—or anyhow, other—conditions have gone on blooming and been, finally, worshiped in rotten ways, was good-and-dead. *Look Homeward, Angel.* God knows we did.

As an adolescent I could feel all this, too. It was there, and not always on the rim of consciousness, either; it was what you lived with, it was what was helping to form the way you would write, what you would write. An affirmer? Yes, and what is critically labeled a romanticist. In the depression I saw with younger eyes—but they saw as well as they do now—miraculous kindness rising from the ash-colored, negation-colored, poverty-smashed winter streets. I knew from the straight-speaking mouth of a teacher of high-school literature classes what fire and wisdom were ours: ours to take, to use, to sing or to speak with. Everything in my life, every racial and waking and known memory began to move and function together in me. I suppose this happens to every novelist. And I suppose it always happens in different ways.

Ours has been called—not with reference to the novel alone, and with some justice—the Age of Criticism. But I can't agree. I don't believe it is any special age; only part of many ages, doing its best. And I am not afraid that it will degenerate into an age of scholarship without creation. What if the eyes of well meaning critics have begun looking too closely at one another's work, blinkered through their own zeal? From my own standpoint, being the owner of a pulse that beats regularly, and a pair of ears that, like any novel-writing animal's, cock to windward for the least trace of danger, I think even the critics of critics of critics do some good, and at their most daisy-chain involution are harmless. Like every novelist, I have to keep remembering and keep in constant touch with things that are, to me, more important: I have to remember what I am, where I came from, and to use what I have with at least the greatest skill I can summon at that moment.

I have to learn when to drop out of self-consciousness, into another level of work where everything is direct, naked, formed and aimed toward a total effect. I have to know the effect is a truth. When the tensions of the world sit roosting on my shoulders, I have to summon sense enough to knock them off; I have to not simply recall, but know, that joy and grief are woven fine, as they were when William Blake knew it; to laugh as I use the fact of laughter.

To statements such as *Ours is the Age of Criticism* I may pay attention, all right, but part of me is busy somewhere else; it is attentive to whispers that come out of the living past, like mocking smoke left from recent campfires. After a while I can distinguish the words being whispered. They are spoken by those relatives who told me family stories and legends and sometimes apocryphal, sometimes factual tales, when I was three and four and then five and able to read. "Listen. This is the story of the wolves that got in the corral where your Great-Grandfather Alpheus used to keep the deer. It was a hard, shiny winter night. . . ."

And: "You want to hear about Dorcas and the Indians again? She was a little girl then, not like your great-grandma now.

Her father died, in the midst of winter, and Dorcas and the boy, Joe, and her mother buried him in dark night, right behind the cabin, deep, with rocks over the grave so the Indians wouldn't know he was gone . . . rocks and brush, and there by night they made it look natural. And then one morning Dorcas was just coming back up the path to the cabin, from the log house, and there before her stood the tallest Indian ever born. . . ."

Or it is the voice of my grandfather, telling about the fine pack of hounds he used to own, telling of them on 'coon hunts on foggy autumn nights in Indiana: "Now, Ruby had the best tongue; ah, she had the purtiest beller. . . ."

Like a huge tapestry shaking in the past, fabric worn but the colors of the threads undimmed, the world of legend that can be put into letters begins to burn. The reality is close now, and so is the past. Very close is everything that can be captured. The novel's strength can bring meaning to banality, life to dust.

Or again it is the voice of D. H. Lawrence: *To be alive, to be whole man alive: that is the point. And at its best, the novel, and the novel supremely, can help you. It can help you not to be a dead man in life.*

When I hear voices like those, everything in me tunes to the same key, and a certain knowledge that began early and had to do with the importance of books, the novel, in everyman's life, is complete.

Sometimes, for a while, when I am trying too hard, or feel angry at the world—or sections of the world—the brightness of the stars about the sky seems cold, actively belligerent. But then in a little while the whole thing changes—I can sit down, and simply start writing, out of the need to be back there writing, the need to say some things that should be said. And at these times I know, without telling myself in so many words, that I have learned a little. I have learned to throw all the armor away, till

I can hear it clang in some dusty corner. I have learned that, even though I may never catch the ghosts I want to catch, I can at least make a hard attempt, putting everything I have into the chase. I have learned that writing a novel is, for me, necessary; between novels, which is never long, I writhe inwardly and have a good many cutting points to make about the mine-run of best-sellers. But, really in the work, in it up to my neck, I can understand that all these gripe sessions are unimportant. Who cares if well packaged and neatly advertised fluff is "seriously" discussed by the lady down the block who happens to adore historicals when they contain blond, bare-chested pirates, or that it is her considered opinion that anybody as funny as I am in conversation ought to write a real masterpiece of humor, maybe something light and satiric about the Navy, Army, or Marines? I think some time I shall indeed write a novel about the Army, and I think it will be funny; it will also be savage, and it will not snuggle up to the happy brass for comfort.

But I don't care about the best-seller-smitten lady, not when I'm writing. Nor do I care much, then, about things that may pester the devil out of me when I am not working through a new novel. The blatant anti-intellectualism of the present administration isn't, in the long run, much worse than that of Harding's. It would be nice to have an impious Mencken around again, poking sharp holes in dull walls, but he was in essence a joyful iconoclast, not one of the great sustainers, and it is, really, sustenance we need—the kind that has nothing to do with local or national politics, but a lot to do with the individual. When I am writing I am more aware than at other times; less bothered by trivia. I have to admit that headlines fall under the category of trivia, at these working times. What I am aware of is a certain motion of existence, a certain authority in the world that makes the meaning of taking a breath important, a humming awareness of everyone I have ever known, and many people I have not known. It isn't far from the feeling of that boy walking into the Gary Public Library, smelling the rich scents of the books, reaching for books, knowing that here is destiny. And yet it is a long distance from him—longer than it is in terms of years—in terms of judgment.

The beautiful part of reading is knowing what to look for, and the beautiful part of writing is knowing what you have to write. Judgment began for me around seventeen when I left school for good and went to work in the Carnegie-Illinois steel mills. I lived then in Hobart, Indiana, twenty or so miles from Gary, and worked the night shift for three years, 11:00 P.M. till 7:00 A.M., Saturday nights off. By that time I had read a lot. I had found Stephen Vincent Benét and Willa Cather and Thomas Wolfe and James Gould Cozzens and Joseph Conrad and Henry James and D. H. Lawrence and Scott Fitzgerald. And I had started to write—not the free-and-easy, free-wheeling sort of writing I had done early in school and early for myself out of school, but writing aimed at teaching myself all I could. In the mornings, when I got home from work, I dug the steel dust out of ears and eyes and sat down at a typewriter and began. I wrote until well into the afternoons, got three or four hours of sleep, got up at six, ate quickly, and worked at writing for a few more hours until it was time to leave for the long drive to work. At work I kept a couple of books in my lunchpail, a nice big fat one, and during the lunch half-hour I crawled up on a pile of waste in the toolroom of the machine shop and read while I ate sandwiches. The rats were thick in the mills in those days; they loved the grease in the roller pits; and when one would come near me in the toolroom I would see the motion of his snout out of the corner of an eye and, as if absently, pick up a heavy bolt and shy it at him, without missing a line of prose. I don't remember what my favorite prose was then. *War and Peace* was

33

a popular novel with me, but I don't think I could have crammed it into the lunchpail.

Saturdays I took off from learning to write. Hobart was a good town. The library wasn't much, but the people were, and the trees and the river were splendid. The river, curving down through the middle of town, gave just enough clearance for a boat to go under the arched bridges if you lay down belly-flat in the boat and paddled with your hands in the black, cold, green-glinting water. There was a moment as you went in under the bridge that was always like the complete faith, the jump-off into blackness, I have felt when starting a novel—and then at the other side you would roll out into light, tons of light, breathing easier and glad you had tried it under the bridge. Going downriver, where there were twists and turns and heavy brush along the banks and birds sitting still in the brush, was like passing into another time, another land that was still in the center of America—it was nice to think, with loving care and in detail, about a girl or girls, to wonder how you could put them in a novel, and to be floating along without sound except for a little hustle of wind over the tops of the thick, overarching trees. In the autumns the water was another color, even blacker but now a smoky black, and there were mats of corncobs floating like red and yellow islands near where the gristmills still operated. It was a good time, the whole three years, a long learning time.

Whatever I have written, I have always gone back to that place and started out from there. Some time I shall write a novel about Hobart, too, but of course it won't be about Hobart; it will only have that feeling in it. It was a time of finding out that I could trust myself, that I could just move straight ahead, in a line of work dictated by the shape of the first sentence, and begin saying things that burst out of me. I wrote a novel, not liking it but liking parts of it very much, and set it aside and without looking at it wrote another one, using the same theme.

34

The second one was better. I took the second one into Chicago, where I had to go to see a fine girl anyhow, on a warm Saturday night, and she joined me; then we went to the Palmer House, where, a squib in the newspaper had said, a certain editor would be in the city for a certain time, inviting new writers to bring in manuscripts so he could take a look at them. I was a new writer, I qualified. He was pouch-eyed and sweating in the dark Chicago heat; a harried man, but courteous, there at the first. I, on the other hand, was exactly as hard as Dempsey in his prime, and I looked good in a white summer suit, and the girl has always been beautiful. The editor, sitting among stacks of manuscript, all of which looked pitiful to me, thumbed through mine; once in a while his lips pursed and he made small noncommittal nosies, "Urg," "Ahp," "Yi!" and "Mh-mmmmmp." Finally he looked up. He stabbed a sentence with his finger. "This man," he said. "You say his head *hit* the pillow. What you mean is, it touched the pillow, or landed lightly on the pillow."

"No," I said. "I mean his head hit the pillow. He was tired. It hit the pillow good and hard. Give me the manuscript."

So I wasn't going to be published for a while, not by that house anyhow, but I felt wonderful, going down in the elevator with the girl, and stepping out on Wabash into the close, quick, adventurous night. I felt fine and I knew what I knew.

In those years I discovered quickly, as ice in the spring light rushes from a stream at the end of a mean winter, that the life of humanity could get into what I did, and I was more than happy in this awareness. I thought I had been observant before that, but now I was ten times quicker to see. I could see that in my own life—I had been shunted from place to place, known a number of backgrounds—there had been nuances of talk, bits of scenes, that could bring into what I did the whole fragrance of other people's lives: and after a while I wasn't as swift to place blame as I had been, but thought, and groped, toward the source of the evil that I had formerly blamed on circumstances and individuals. I rediscovered what I had, for a while, forgotten, the joy of writing for the fun of it, as a child runs barefoot in the sun. And at the same time I had intimations of the future: of the fact that I would never be done with learning about people, and that every time I learned something more about them I would know that much more about myself. In those years I was like the Greeks who came to the sea, and saw it shining, and shouted, "The sea! The sea!" and laughed and waded into it, the tears of their emotion streaming over their faces, mixing with their beards.

I still feel the same way; the vision has grown this far, and I believe it will go on growing, burning away, getting stronger. Sometimes when I get up from the desk after a night's work I feel kinship that is solid as that shared among men who have just come out of battle, a feeling that embraces the entire world: quietly, with knowing that goes beyond the reach of cleverness or craft or skill. But the craft and skill have to be there too, part of the need to make others know the exact way it was. I have had a few idols topple from pedestals and lie in shards; I thank them anyhow for what I got from them, and do not blame them for not staying idols, being better writers than they were. The surfaces of many styles that I have admired now stand as surfaces only; I can understand the pressures that pushed too hard on their owners, money-pressures, woman-pressures, life-pressures, so that the styles turned to just bright textures over bones.

But the names I knew first as guides are still there: Benét and Conrad and James and Cozzens and Forster and Lawrence and Wolfe and Fitzgerald. In this Sunday's paper I see that a new genius has been acclaimed; this one has ripped the roofs off a small town, showing with violence never before equaled the pettiness and squalor and fornication and chicanery inside. I look over a reviewer's long excerpt: somehow it sounds drab and mechanical, inorganic. Fornication ought at any rate to be fun. I pick up a copy of *The Ordeal of Mark Twain*, and suddenly find myself laughing, slinging it across the room, and going over to take Huck Finn off the shelf. Emerson said if you aim at a king you must kill him. If you set out to make a martyr you'd better prove it.

The vision has taught me a few other things too, at this stage of the game—when to give everything I have, when to hold back. And after many broils in a thousand arenas it has also made me understand that I can't give any real anxiety to over-literary problems that simmer down to so much fribbling on the fringe of truth. I read constantly and whenever I can, when I am not writing. Poets who were once just persuasive music-makers say more to me with each reading. Often I have a sense of oneness with earth, being in the right place at the right time. Often, too, I am haunted on the edge of night-sleep or in early morning by a conviction that I have seen and talked with someone in another time. And when I have felt the Power of the Hand on me I know, each time, that it will always come back. The vision stays alive. From it I know that my restlessness when not writing, the prowling feeling when my mind flicks hungrily around a thousand outside events, will be something I'll get over. I shall learn the hard way, as I have learned everything, that when it is necessary to stop writing, for a little time, the action can wait, be dormant like a seeded field under rain. The brain can stir with green shoots that may have only nebulous form but are moving even while the front of the brain is occupied with other matters.

From the vision then to the vision now I have learned things harder to analyze. For instance, that *The Rainbow* is a greater novel than *Sons and Lovers;* but I can't pin down why I know this, except to say it tries harder, ranges more widely, accepts more fully. I can't pin it down because I am not, in the critical sense, a critic: I know this novel and a hundred more better than any critic; I do not know them in critical parlance, but with intimacy—as a man knows a woman, as a farmer knows a field he loves. Intimacy never asks questions.

That is the way the vision works; without question, sharpening elements of understanding, making the hands try to reach more than they have before. It is the most quick and constant fact I know, going right along with the joys of flesh and spirit. When it heats and shines I am again the boy in the library, and I am the man at the typewriter too. I can feel the great curve of what has been said, of what can be said, moving up like light from many pages.

John Brooks

Some Notes on Writing One Kind of Novel

P ROBABLY one of the few things on which all contemporary American novelists would agree is that the conditions in which they live are less than perfect for the practice of their craft. Their economic woes, in the first place, are tiresomely well known. The chances of making a decent living at novel writing alone are so poor, and the tax structure is so badly stacked against a person whose income is capricious, that practically all of them resort to other means of making money part time. Of course, jackpots for the novelist exist, and they sometimes go to good books, but to put the matter crudely, you generally decrease your chance of winning them when you write as well as you can. I think it is safe to say that, unless he is particularly given to self-delusion, no serious novelist is in the business, rather than in some other, primarily for profit.

For fame, then? Perhaps in part, but fame, even in rosy prospect, is not an unmixed blessing to a man or woman of novelist's temperament; he can analyze too acutely the destruction that fame has wreaked on others of his time, in terms of lost privacy, overinflated ego, demands on time, disruption of family life, and so on, to contemplate the prospect of being famous without a certain feeling of queasiness. Well, what about critical acclaim— the approval of a presumably select and discriminating few? It is true that there are kind words for almost any novel that gets into print to be found in one or another of the popular review media, and it is equally true that in certain limited circles the serious contemporary novel is followed, heralded, and greeted with an eagerness bordering on the hysterical; but in general, the fact is that among many critics at the present time the novel is getting to be an object of contumely. "The novel," Yvor Winters wrote in a recent issue of *Hudson Review*, "for the most part an abortive form from its beginnings, is dying rapidly." The statement is stamped, somehow, with the bland shape of a truism so familiar as to be wearisome; without arguing the question of whether the form used by Fielding and Thackeray, Tolstoi and Dostoevski, Stendhal and Flaubert, Hemingway and Faulkner can properly be termed abortive, I wish merely to call attention to the casual tone of the statement, implying that no argument is expected. I am aware that this kind of talk has been going on almost as long as there has *been* such a thing as a novel,* but lately it seems to me that the kettledrums of doom in the critical symphony have been building to a crescendo. A couple of winters ago in New York, I remember sitting through a weird session of literary murder-and-suicide, in which a man whose chief occu-

---

* T. S. Eliot wrote in an article on *Ulysses* in 1923, "The novel ended with Flaubert and James." Two years later he wrote to Fitzgerald about *The Great Gatsby*, "It seems to me to be the first step that American fiction has taken since Henry James." It would appear, then, that what is needed to raise the novel from the dead is simply a good novel.

pation is criticizing contemporary fiction announced to a group of practicing novelists, without qualification or apology, that the novel is already dead, beyond any hope of resuscitation by science, art, or prayer. Most everybody there nodded gravely—that's how far the brainwashing has progressed.

However, none of the writers at that meeting gave up their craft as a result of it, and in general, except as it affects their sensibilities or their personal fortunes, I do not think novelists are much concerned about what critics or reviewers say. They are more concerned—money considerations entirely aside—about the reaction of that mysterious entity, the public. The trouble, of course, is that at present there are so many publics. The novelist who is neither an established habitual best-seller nor an academic writing specifically for others of his breed has an odd and fragmentary sense of his audience. He knows, say, that his last book sold seven or eight thousand or even ten thousand copies in the hard-cover edition and has a chance—just a chance—to go into paperbacked reprint and thus eventually reach a quarter of a million people. Of the paperback audience he knows nothing; it is faceless and nameless; it reads books on trains without noticing who the author is; it hardly ever writes him letters. It is of the small hard-cover audience that he catches occasional glimpses. This audience starts with his immediate family and friends, all of whom can be counted on to read his book whether he supplies them with autographed copies of it or not, but few of whom can be counted on to give him an opinion that can be taken at its face value. Apart from them, the most significant glimpse of his audience that he gets is the occasional person he meets by accident at a cocktail party or on a tennis court who has read the book and is willing to tell him so. She is usually a housewife with a college education. (Statistics prove that 96.45 per cent of all readers of novels that sell between five and ten thousand copies fall into this category.) She proceeds to tell him what she liked about the book, and lo! she has picked out the very things that *he* liked best when he put them in, and she has not only understood them but, by talking about them, given them a new dimension. By God! the novelist thinks. If I'd heard what she had to say before the book was written, I could have done it better. And next time I will. Regardless of what may be the subsequent history of his new friendship, the encounter leaves the novelist in a glow. He is not so crazy as to suppose that he has suddenly become famous, although it must be admitted that he now finds himself recalling many things in the almost forgotten book and deciding that it must be as good as he once thought it was rather than as bad as he has been assuming recently. He is now itching to get back to his new book, and that is a condition of spirit and body too rare to be wasted. He has been offered actual contact with a real reader who read his book by choice, and that may be just about as useful to him as any criticism he is ever likely to get.

But the more confusing aspect of the relationship of novelist to contemporary public is the absence of any objective criterion of value. To please one group is to outrage another. The best-seller brings fame and fortune, but, almost *ipso facto*, whatever its merit, it brings its author ostracism among highbrow critics and readers who have a stake in the esoteric. The worst-seller finds the highbrow critics and readers rather predisposed in its favor ("Oh, you read *The Adventures of Augie March?* Well, if you want the *real* Bellow, dig out *The Victim*.") Success is failure; failure is success. In this anarchic situation there is something for everybody, and nothing for anybody. Almost any writer who undergoes the pain and toil of learning his craft decently well and suffering a few initial reverses will probably end up by getting published, and many writers get published over and over again without ever meeting those requirements. So even this rock-bottom criterion has little value.

As if all these were not enough troubles to plague the novelist, the poor fellow practices what must be one of the most exacting and exhausting trades in the world. Writing in itself is seldom really much fun. I know of no one for whom it is a relaxing hobby, as painting or music can be. It is easy to start a novel and easy to end one; but it is hard to write the middle. I would even venture the opinion—in the face, I admit, of overwhelming evidence of all kinds to the contrary—that no one who sets himself any standards to speak of and actually finishes a novel, even a bad or skimpy one, can be a completely unadmirable person. A novel starts with a vision and ends with an interpretation, or a synthesis, of the vision. But there is inevitably a time in the writing of what goes between—I think it is inclined to come between two-thirds and three-quarters of the way through—when continuing with the work at hand ceases to be a painful pleasure and becomes an outright burden. The original vision is temporarily lost; the novel becomes a great, inert weight on the spirit of the writer, a stumbling block before him, ruining his temper and disrupting his sleep. His working hours are now devoted largely to inventing ruses to make work that is hard and distasteful seem easy and pleasant; he tries typing while leaning back in an armchair, he tries taking a pad out in the garden and writing longhand, he tries working after a couple of drinks (fatal). Nothing helps much. Worst of all, in worrying about his Problem (which is his book) he forgets that his characters are people; he manipulates them cruelly and arbitrarily for the sake of getting on with the book; where a hundred pages earlier he exulted or suffered with their every action, now he can make a character do a terrible thing without feeling any compunction whatever. He has lost touch; his nerves and his book are in wrecks. It is in this terrain on the weedy trail of novel writing that the men are separated from the boys. The attics of America are full of two-thirds-written novels. But if what is needed—will or compulsion—is there, the work somehow goes on, and finally the bad time

43

passes. Of course, what was written during it will have to be entirely rewritten later, when the vision has been rekindled, changed, and enlarged. The work of writing a novel involves not only the revisions one hears so much about, but many re-visions, too.

Add to the difficulties I have mentioned, one more—the current state of the world. As this is written, Soviet tanks stand in the streets of Budapest and British ones in Port Said; next week the crisis will be somewhere else, and all the while the hydrogen bombs are cached away, ready for instant arming, at God knows what jet air bases. Every night's news is a new drama more arresting than all but the most sensational fiction. In these times even a novel that tries to go straight to the bottom of the human predicament in its current manifestation must seem a little like needlework.

Is this what is meant by the death of the novel? Perhaps; yet thousands of new novels are published every year, and they are selected from tens of thousands submitted; evidently the needlework goes on, and on a rather massive scale. Why, then, this obsessive fiddling with an abortive old form? What's it all about?

I am sure that the answer is that there are many answers. A form broad enough to embrace *Tristram Shandy* and *Madame Bovary*, *Pride and Prejudice* and *Finnegans Wake*, needs practitioners with many different motives. Faulkner said when he accepted the Nobel Prize that novelists must get back to what he considers the only right subject, "the human heart in conflict with itself." Novelists whose work is predominantly lyrical are, I suppose, motivated by the poets' age-old need to express the inexpressible (and if the obstacles in a novelist's way in the present world are large, those in the way of a poet are nothing less than mountainous). Probably a novelist can testify meaningfully only for himself. Speaking for myself, then, I am able to say that one reason for writing the novel is to satisfy a passion to record. That

44

nothing should be lost, that the essences of one's time as well as its facts and figures should be set down, that the timeless struggles of the human heart should be seen exactly as they existed under a certain set of conditions—such is the aim and also the motive for writing of one type of contemporary novelist. Or perhaps I should say of one contemporary novelist.

Such a novelist must admit at the outset that he shoots at smaller game than those whose target is to discover and enunciate new human truths. Nonetheless, he is sure that if his aim is true, what his marksmanship brings home will be something of permanent interest. His *primary* target—and I have to stress "primary" because practically all novelists have in common certain goals such as the creation of believable characters and the telling of a believable and interesting story—is a journalistic one. Indeed, his aim is almost identical with that of some of the best journalism, except that the novelist tries to go somewhat further: he tries to filter the facts and attitudes and people of his time through his own personality (which is itself a product of his time) to a greater degree than is ordinarily possible in journalism, and, by way of enhancing his tale's meaning, to take advantage of freedom from the trammels of fact. He never alters facts merely to improve his story; only to heighten it. He asks himself, Can I find a way to have it happen that is *truer* than the way it actually happened? Perhaps not; and if not, he is not prejudiced against using chunks of reality whole. Chief among his premises are that social behavior, as well as individual behavior, is an aspect of the human heart, and an interesting one; and that the uniformity of the many presents a dramatic background against which to project the individuality of a few. He is ever alert to the comic possibilities of social behavior; indeed, although he need not by any means wear the comic mask all the time, he always has it ready to slip on at a moment's notice. The sort of novel he aims to write might be called the social novel, had not that term been preempted to describe a group of books written chiefly during the thirties and having a distinct ethical and political bias. It could be called the novel of society, but only at the risk of suggesting, incorrectly, that its setting is invariably the likes of upper Fifth Avenue or Monaco. It is close to the old novel of manners, but manners have changed so much in the past fifty years that the term would be limiting and actually misleading. Therefore I'll speak of it as the recording novel; and in case that sounds too temporary and mortal, it may be well to recall Turgenev's *Fathers and Sons*, a recording novel about a specific and idiosyncratic society now nearly a century gone that shows as well as any the permanence of interest attainable within this form.

I have spoken of the novel as beginning with a vision and I have spoken of the passion to record. Both the vision and the passion are essential. The vision in the recording novel must, I think, be a vision of a certain place at a certain time, taken out of the author's experience. Other novelists may begin with a character, a situation, or even a theme. The writer I seek to explain begins with the feeling he had the time he was standing at dawn in a field on a hazy morning, or the time he discovered late at night that he was locked inside an office building in the middle of a great city, or the time he returned to the town of his boyhood and, standing in a cloud of bus exhaust on a crowded streetcorner, remembered the sound of horses' hoofs on cobblestones after midnight. And he thinks, If I can find a way to trap everything I saw and felt at that certain moment—if I can set down exactly how it was, in every shade and implication—I shall have made a permanent and meaningful statement about my time as a whole. Finding the way is the problem of writing the novel that then begins. People and a story come next, and they must be real people and a real story; but somehow, if the whole thing works, if some chemical interaction occurs between the people and story and the setting which was the starting point, then the people and story will grow out of themselves and become somewhat larger than life. As for theme—well, it's best to let that take care of itself. Start with a theme, and you find you have created a lecture.

The stamp of its beginnings will remain in the novel to the end. If the novel is successful—by which I mean, if the interaction occurs—the discerning reader will, in the course of reading it, experience something very much like what the writer has experienced in his moment of truth in the field or the office building or the town. If he is of an analytical turn of mind he may be able, on reflection, to deduce the very experience that has given rise to the book (although such analysis is irrelevant to his appreciation of it). For example, I am sure that *The Great Gatsby* must have been conceived, consciously or unconsciously, at dawn on Long Island one summer morning, in the gray-turning, gold-turning light; at the break of a cool, pleasant day, when the lawn still looked blue and the birds suddenly sang with harsh cheerfulness and last night's party was not quite over yet. Everything in the book is built artfully around the feeling of this scene, which is the key scene of the plot and the turning point in the life of the title character. The scene is not the novel; it is the starting point of the novel. Without the rest, the scene itself is nothing, or nothing but a suggestive vignette; and yet without the scene and the feeling it evokes, plot and characters would add up to nothing but melodrama.

So much for the vision; now for the passion. For passion must be there, anger or love or nostalgia or even hatred. In speaking of "recording" I have perhaps implied auctorial disinterestedness, or at least the posture spoken of at literary teas as dégagé. If so, incorrectly. I like John Peale Bishop's statement that the novel should tell the "moral history" of the novelist's time. Moral it must be to have life, because life is so largely a matter of morals. The recording novelist's attitude toward his material can be anything from downright approval through amusement and skepticism all the way to Swiftian savage indignation. Perhaps the latter end of the spectrum more often makes for better novels than the former; but the important thing is that the novelist have an attitude that he is sure of and that it be implicit, but only implicit, in what he writes. Let him think of himself as a photographer—let him be content to deal with material about which he is so indifferent that he *can* think that way—and he is lost.

A superficial view might be that a satire of manners is an amoral affair in which the writer merely laughs at various forms of human posturing without presuming to judge. To this I retort that to the very extent that it is concerned with manners, the recording novel is concerned with morals. For what are most manners but a conscientious effort to do the right thing, and what is that but morality, however misdirected? The novelist making sport of a housewife keeping up with the Joneses or a tycoon using the wrong fork is inevitably judging them, harshly or charitably, according to the context. The opposite poles of fiction, the points between which the needle of fashion swings as generations succeed each other, are sensibility and morality; a novel must be oriented strongly toward one pole or the other. (All bets are off in the case of such an all-embracing masterpiece as *Remembrance of Things Past*.) The recording novelist is committed to the moral pole. Descriptions of manners are without life and color unless the writer has, and has the skill to imply, an attitude toward the manners; he must think they are ridiculous or commendable or contemptible or merely human, or combinations of these. Otherwise, he presents nothing but a tape recording—material for a novel by somebody who has the necessary passion. Many such tape recordings pass for novels in our time, and if what is recorded happens to surprise or shock enough people, their parrot-like authors are hailed for a few weeks as geniuses. But a year or two later, when the newsy bloom is off the events described, the books are dead.

The moral commitment of the recording novelist is also his great limitation; that is, if he wants his work to have impact and if he isn't Proust, he must largely reject the vast equipment of modern psychology in presenting and explaining his characters, because psychology points straight to the sensibility pole. His interest in psychology is as a social phenomenon, not as a method of approach to human character. Its prevalence in the conversation and thought of his contemporaries is his material, not his weapon. His characters must be presumed to be, up to a certain point, free and responsible agents—a status that modern psychology tends to deny them—or else he cannot possibly be interested in them. "Susan Kenny had always been jealous of her younger sister." "Hank Thompson seldom got through a business day without feeling the urge to punch his employer on the nose." Thus the novelist interested in manners states a psychological condition in the sentence with which he begins his chapter, instead of analyzing it in a ten-thousand-word flashback. He does not tell how the condition came about, but rather what happens as a result of it, and his chapter is about how those old emotions, jealousy and hatred, however caused, acted on the people who harbored them, and on others, at a certain time and place in the world's history.

So the idea that all human actions are determined either by environment or by early childhood experiences is an uncongenial one, if not actually anathema, to our novelist, and I think it may be added that he finds modern psychology humorless, dull, and finally unsatisfactory as a way of accounting for human conduct, the roots of which he prefers to let remain a mystery. He accepts human idiosyncrasy at its face value rather than thinking of it as a symptom or a syndrome. At the same time, he suffers from the limitation of viewpoint he imposes on himself. He is subject to the influence of the currents of psychological thought that are in the air, and almost inevitably he sometimes lets the influence creep into his work, corrupting it. Then he wonders what is wrong: Why does page fifty-six seem to fall apart? Why do the bones seem to break just there? And he discovers that he has inadvertently begun psychoanalyzing Susan, the very thing that, to make his book self-consistent, he must not do. He cuts out the lapse, but with misgivings; after all, he thinks, Susan *is* neurotic and I *do* understand, up to a point, the cause of her neurosis. Nevertheless, for the sake of his art the passage must go. After such a novelist has plied his trade for several books he may find himself abandoning the rock on which he has stood, and, in a sort of orgy, writing a purely psychological novel, one oriented toward sensibility. It is a bad novel, because in writing it he has plied not his own trade but someone else's. I imagine many good novelists have one such excursion into an unfamiliar milieu either in print, quite properly neglected, or in the trunk as a result of either the writer's own prudent second thoughts or his publisher's prudent refusal to publish it. This failure has its uses to the novelist: it represents the practical proof that for the sake of art he must do what all of us, in art or living, must do to act effectively— that is, commit oneself consciously to a partial view of life.

If my impression is correct, the kind of novel I have been speaking of is considered by the reigning critics to be somewhat deader than the general average. It was not ever thus; as few as thirty years ago, the recording novel had a high degree of critical acceptance, and reached a high degree of achievement. Isn't our knowledge of the mood and spirit, the moral weather, of the twenties far richer for *The Sun Also Rises* and *The Great Gatsby?* Critics have since canonized these books by investing them with all sorts of myths and symbols; but what they began and ended with was their authors' effort to set down exactly how it was. Both authors were superbly successful; hundreds of others of that period were less so, in varying degrees.

Since then this kind of novel has had several ups and downs; at present it seems to be suffering from the fragmentation that has been happening to the arts in general in America of recent years. I hope I have made it sufficiently clear that when I speak of the recording novel I do not mean that postwar popular favorite, the naturalistic one—the one that gains its temporary interest from its mere mention of places and subjects and issues with which we are temporarily concerned; the one, in short, that tells not how it was but what it was. I mean, instead, a work that passes the era through an individual sensibility so that the effect, if not creative in the truest sense of that battered word, is *re*-creative. Since the end of the Second World War the vogue of the purely naturalistic novel has caused a violent reaction in the other direction among writers of sensitivity and artistic aspiration. The result is that the recording novel, which properly exists somewhere between the extremes of naturalism and mandarinism, has tended to be left high and dry. This fragmentation, I suppose, is paralleled in the visual arts by the rapid movement of so many painters toward more and more opaque abstraction, in reaction against a generation during which we have seen photography—technique produced by a machine—come to be regarded as potentially a high art form.

Returning to the novel in more specific terms: during this century, what with the breakdown of social stratifications and the tremendous advances in technology culminating in the production of weapons capable of destroying the race, the job of recording contemporary social history in depth has become infinitely more complex than it ever was before. With so many facts at hand, people's lust for facts has become practically insatiable, and to meet this new demand journalism has risen to exceptional heights. In the face of this barrage of the particular and the timely, the serious novel's retreat to a world apart has evidently been the result of an impulse to shake off the time's mud and fly up to the universal. But too often the results have been mere academic exercises with very little humanity in them, and the reader has been led to suspect that the novelist's reason for avoiding the here and now was not so much to rise above its limitations as to escape his inability to grasp and impose form upon it.

And along with this avoidance of the compelling material at hand has gone a tendency by many serious writers and critics to rationalize the avoidance. What they would seem to be saying is that the novel of manners cannot be written any more. They look to Henry James (himself, of course, a master novelist of manners); they have made increasingly famous the passage from his life of Hawthorne:

. . . one might enumerate the items of high civilization, as it exists in other countries, which are absent from the texture of American life, until it should become a wonder to know what was left. No State, in the European sense of the word, and indeed barely a specific national name. No sovereign, no court, no personal loyalty, no aristocracy, no church, no clergy, no army, no diplomatic service, no country gentlemen, no palaces, nor castles, nor manors, nor old country houses, nor parsonages, nor thatched cottages, nor ivied ruins; no cathedrals, nor abbeys, nor little Norman churches; no great Universities nor public schools—no Oxford, nor Eton, nor Harrow; no literature, no novels, no museums, no pictures, no political society, no sporting class—no Epsom nor Ascot!

None, indeed! And, responding to the elegiac tone of this writer whose neurotic shrinking from experience was his strength as well as his weakness, the modern critics say that the disintegration of all the things James mourned has progressed in America much further since his time, to the point where no trace of the old standards and their symbols is any longer present. What is needed is a fixed, stratified society to project character against. America has no such society. No manors, no manners! Hence, no novels of manners.

My suggestion is that the exact opposite is true. The job of the novelist of manners has simply become more complex, more challenging, and more important. *Haven't* we got now in America, after all, a society that is worth writing about, and if not, why is everyone else in the world so interested in us, not only in our foreign policy and its largesse but in our smallest ways, our overheated rooms and the changing of our knife and fork from hand to hand to cut our meat? Who can say that we don't act in certain definable ways, just as the people with kings, manors, and country gentlemen did, and that our ways can't be made, in fiction, to appear funny, sad, touching, and illuminating—everything that the novel of manners should be? Other-directedness can be satirized as well as tradition-directedness; there is as much humor in the ways of Jamaica as of Ascot, as much poignancy in the lack of security fostered by income taxes and bombs as in the security ensured by primogeniture. Life, in short, goes on, and it is still lived by people, who are what the novel is all about. If our present society is more varied and complex than was Victorian England's, and if the novelist's job in describing it is so much the harder, surely that isn't a reason to throw up our hands and give the novel up as a bad job. If we do that, we are leaving the describing of one of the most interesting periods in the world's history to pollsters, formal journalists, naturalistic novelists, and sociologists. There is something to be added to what any of them can say.

Not the least of the jobs of the contemporary novelist is that of rescuing American society from the charge that it doesn't exist.

Having found himself with the odd vocation to write novels, the American writer faces a problem almost as pressing as the choice of subject matter: How should he live? It is not entirely an economic problem, although economics are certainly near its core. There are essentially three ways: he may teach, he may hole up in the city or the country and do nothing but write novels, or he may divide his time between novel writing and some more consistently lucrative business or profession. Each of the solutions has its advantages and disadvantages. The academy provides an intellectually stimulating milieu, and one in which the novelist's work will surely be read thoughtfully and appreciatively by people with whom he is in daily contact. On the other hand, the milieu provided tends to be something of a hothouse one, and in addition there is some evidence that the academic novelist is under overwhelming pressure, if he desires the approval of his peers and academic and social advancement, to restrict whatever talents he may have to the production of a certain kind of novel, rather formal and bloodless. And there is the fact that after a time, much of what he knows is the campus; you can go just so far writing novels about *that*. The second method—being a novelist and nothing but a novelist—is practiced by only a courageous few, and crown them all with bay leaves for their sheer gall! Their position has all the obvious advantages—complete independence, full time to devote to their work, the theoretical freedom to live anywhere they want. In practice, though, the full-time novelist's freedom of action is often restricted by various factors, external and internal to himself. For one thing, the struggle for economic survival may keep him writing books at a rate that is faster than his natural one. To get out a book a year, he must all too often go back to work before the emotional well has filled up again—he must produce "with forced fingers rude." Secondly, the nothing-but-novelist is artificially isolated from his material. He sees a small circle of friends, most of whom are too often connected in one way or another with writers, writing, or publishing; he spends his four hours a day at his desk; he is in the happy position of being able to spend far more time with his wife and children than the average American; when he finishes a book he gets a sitter for the kids and is off for a two-week driving trip with his wife, before getting back to the old portable and writing "Chapter I"

54

again. Not a bad life; but in terms of his work he may suffer from the fact that it has no organic connection either with the "uptown" world of organized struggle for social status or with the "downtown" world of organized struggle for economic status. As far as society is concerned, he operates in a vacuum. It is interesting in this connection to note that Ernest Hemingway found the material for what many still consider his best book specifically in his experiences as a newspaperman in Paris and Spain. In his later works, which he has been able to write as a nothing-but-novelist, many have noted a certain thinness of material and a detachment from the social texture he had shown himself so good at creating. And my third criticism of the life of the nothing-but-novelist is simply that if he is less successful than Hemingway he may become embittered at society; he may become a victim of what one such writer has described to me as "justifiable paranoia." This ailment may be productive of a funny or lively book or two, but ultimately it will blight not only his life but his work as well.

There remains the third category, the novelists who have some regular occupation other than novel writing or teaching. The advantage here, of course, is freedom from the need to make a living at novel writing, and the disadvantage is lack of time. The other occupation may be law or insurance or business, but very often—for the obvious reason that most writers can sell their time at the best price by writing—it is journalism. There are additional disadvantages here. Journalism is particularly time-consuming and emotionally exhausting, if undertaken seriously; its over-all demands on a writer, in fact, are practically equal to those of fiction writing. Journalism and novel writing, furthermore, are almost exact opposites as to point of view. A novelist-journalist wastes many painful weeks in the process of changing gears either way, and so far as I know or can learn from my colleagues who straddle these two occupations, no mental or emotional automatic transmission for their use has yet been developed in Detroit or elsewhere. The man who has some other occupation that will use other lobes of his brain and leave the writing lobes fresh, or even refresh them, is the luckiest of all. Failing this, for the novelist interested in the kind of novel I have spoken of, I think the fiction-journalism straddle is the most natural one. For one thing, his journalistic work keeps him stirring around, uptown and down, and thus in rare touch with his material. For another, he likes it; because even in his fiction he is, by design, part journalist.

Having completed a catalogue of hardships, I now wish to state that I consider the conditions for the production of good novels in America over the next twenty years or so to be generally excellent. You may ask, for heaven's sake, why? Well, I reply, Dr. Edmund Bergler, the psychoanalyst noted for breaking writers' blocks, has explained to us novelists in his books that we are all masochists. Since we are masochists, will we not be most productive when we are regularly whipped?

I am somewhat less than half serious about that. Still, the present situation does have its advantages: in particular, the confusion of audiences and the confusion of critical standards. In the Old World system of literary café and coterie life, even a mediocre writer may well feel warm and loved, confident of who his appreciative audience is; so he goes on his self-assured way, believing that he is thinking when he is only parroting, or that he is feeling when he is only hoking up sentiment—happily unaware of his mediocrity. In America there comes a time in every novelist's development—and I think it is likely to come rather early—when he realizes that the literary world in his country, far more than the social world, is in a state of anarchy; that no matter how good his work is, it will be blamed and scorned by some or, contrariwise, that if he deliberately makes it as bad as he can—ungrammatical, platitudinous, sentimental, sadistic, a deliberate affront to all taste and every decent human standard—it will be wildly praised by some; that, in short, virtually all critical and public opinion is, so far as he is concerned, only a medley of voices out of a void. Thus he is forced early to the ultimate discipline of self-appraisal; and thus, with luck or prayer, to do the best work he is capable of.

Ralph Ellison
Society, Morality, and the Novel

SURELY IT would be of more value for a novelist
to write novels than to spend his energies discussing The Novel, for by carrying out his chosen task there he has
the possibility of moving beyond the given level of either his
talent or his cold perception of life's meaning—of "playing beyond his game," as it were, and thus achieving for himself and
for his readers some new insight into the human predicament,
some new facet of human possibility. By risking the unknown
which appears whenever he follows the lead of his imagination
as driven by his hopes and his fears, he has the chance of achieving
the significantly new and thus becoming himself a part of that
which he achieves. While on the other hand, theorizing about the
form, function, and *raison d'être* of the novel leads him straight-
way into the fields of social and aesthetic criticism, the domain
of specialists. Here he is held in by rules which are alien to his

obsessive need to play with the fires of chaos and to rearrange reality to the patterns of his imagination. For while it is the drive of the critic to create systems of thought, it is that of the novelist to re-create reality in the forms which his personal vision assumes as it plays and struggles with the vividly illusory "eidetic-like" imagery left in the mind's eye by the process of social change. Life for him is a game of hide-and-seek in which he is eternally the sometimes delighted but more often frustrated "it."

Critics are, on the whole, more "adult" types. They share a liking for order and have little patience with dashing about trying to pin down the multiple illusions projected by life with arbitrary ones of one's arrogant own; it is their function to dispense with that annoying characteristic of life with the bright pure light of their methods. The novelist must take chances or die, while the critic would make it unnecessary to do so. Critics would give you the formula that would make the achievement of a major fiction as certain as making a pre-mixed apple pie. They analyze, they classify, they man the lines of continuity linking up present developments with past achievements of the form; and, with their specialized knowledge, they compose the novelists' most sensitively aware audience—or so we have long been accustomed to regarding them. Presently we shall take a closer look at just how contemporary fiction criticism mediates between the American novelist and the American reader, but here let us simply observe that novelists have, for the most part, been content to keep out of the critics' domain. They either confine those critical formulations necessary to the clarification of their own artistic purposes to their notebooks, or they have used them to give substance to occasional book reviews. Most often they have merely played them out by ear as they went about composing specific works of fiction. And for good reason.

Actually, the best way for a novelist to discuss the problem of The Novel is in the form of *a specific novel,* for whenever fictional technique makes conjunction with an image of reality each is mutually transformed. Every serious novel is, beyond its immediate thematic preoccupations, a discussion of the craft, a conquest of the form, and a conflict with its difficulties; a pursuit of its felicities and beauty. To engage in this by way of getting at specific aspects of experience is enough to do, and difficult enough to do, to keep the novelists busy; but today, with some of our more important critics handing down the death sentence of the form (for in their solemn, "The novel is dead," there sounds a Platonist, "*Let* it be dead"), or when they boast left-handedly in print of their loss of interest in contemporary novels, the novelist is feinted into a position of defending his craft. If he is to pay the critics the serious attention which certainly a few of them deserve, and if he is at all interested in winning those readers who would listen to the critics, he is moved to attempt some broad public formulation of his personal approach to his craft. One writes because one wishes to be read on one's own terms; thus, since the critics dismiss the novel as moribund, a bit of explicit communication between the novelist and his prospective readers is most in order. He must prepare to play Antony to the novel's Caesar, for truly an act of assassination has been commissioned. Nor is this all, for a question of personal dignity and rationality is raised. For if the critics are correct, and some are so persuaded, how then does the novelist justify, even to himself, his passionate involvement with a literary form which is dead? Why does he pour his energies into a form that dooms his best efforts to dust even before the effort of the imagination takes place, and upon what does he base his faith?

But first an attempt at definition, which inasmuch as it represents the general assumptions out of which I personally approach the abstract form, will make up for what it lacks in precision with its validity as autobiography.

Let us begin by mentioning a characteristic of the novel which seems so obvious that it is seldom mentioned, and which as a consequence tends to make most discussions of the form irritatingly abstract: By its nature it seeks to communicate a vision of experience. Thus whatever else it achieves artistically, it is basically a form of communication. When successful in communicating its vision of experience, that magic thing occurs between the world of the novel and the reader—and indeed, between reader and reader in their mutual solitude—which we know as communion. For, as with all the fictive arts, the novel's medium of communication consists in a "familiar" experience occurring among a particular people, within a particular society or nation (and the novel is bound up with the notion of nationhood), and it achieves its universality, if at all, through accumulating images of reality and arranging them in patterns of universal significance. It is not, like poetry, concerned primarily with words, but with action depicted in words; and it operates by amplifying and giving resonance to a specific complex of experience until, through the eloquence of its statement, that specific part of life speaks metaphorically for the whole.

The novel can communicate with us only by appealing to that which we "know," through actual experience or through literature, to be the way things occur. "Yes, this is how it is," we tell ourselves when the fictive illusion works its spell; or we say, "Yes, but such and such is left out." Thus between the novelist and his most receptive reader (really a most necessary collaborator who must participate in bringing the fiction into life) there must exist a body of shared assumptions—concerning reality and necessity, possibility and freedom, personality and value—along with a body of feelings, both rational and irrational, which arise from the particular circumstances of their mutual society. Even the technical means through which this collaboration is brought about depends upon the reader's acceptance of a set of artistic conventions, those "once upon a time" devices which announce the telling of a tale and which introduce a mood of receptiveness in the reader and through which alone the novelist is able to bring his fiction alive. Even surrealism depended for its effects upon those who were initiated into its conventions and who shared its assumptions concerning art and value. It is by appealing to our sense of experience and playing upon our shared assumptions that the novelist is able to reveal to us that which we do not know; that is, the unfamiliar within the familiar, and affirm that which we assume to be truth and to reveal to us his own hard-won vision of truth.

In this sense the novel is rhetorical. For whatever else it tries to do, it must do so by persuading us to accept the novelist's projection of an experience which, on some level or mixtures of levels, we have shared with him, and through which we become empathetically involved in the illusory and plotted depiction of life which we identify as fictional art. We repay the novelist in terms of our admiration to the extent that he intensifies our sense of the real—or, conversely, *to the extent that he justifies our desire to evade certain aspects of reality which we find unpleasant beyond the point of confrontation.* In the beginning was not only the word but the contradiction of the word; sometimes we approach life out of a tragic sense of necessity, and again with its denial. In this lies the novel's flexibility and its ability to transcend the bounds of class and nation, its endless possibilities of mutation. It is rooted in man's most permanent feelings and it brings into full vision the processes of his current social forms. This is almost enough in itself to keep the novelist at his task, for in it lies the possibility of affirmation and personal definition.

As an art form the novel is obsessed by the relationship between illusion and reality as revealed in duration, in process. "All poetry," writes Malraux, "implies the destruction of the relationship between things that seems obvious to us in favor of particular relationships imposed by the poet." Thus the novel seeks to take the surface "facts" of experience and arrange them in such ways that for a magic moment reality comes into sharp and significant focus. And I believe that the primary social function of the novel (the function from which it takes its form and which brought it into being) is that of seizing from the flux and flow of our daily lives those abiding patterns of experience which, through their repetition and consequences in our affairs, help to form our sense of reality and from which emerge our sense of humanity and our conception of human value.

More than any other literary form, the novel is obsessed with the impact of change upon personality. Thus it was no mere historical accident that the novel came into prominence during the eighteenth century or that it became fully conscious of itself as an art form during the nineteenth. Its appearance marked the fulfillment of a social need that arose out of the accelerated process of historical change. Before the eighteenth century, when man was relatively at home in what seemed to be a stable and well ordered world (and if not well ordered, stable nevertheless), there was little need for this change-obsessed literary form. Nor was there literacy enough, nor was the individual, tied as he was to an order imposed by religion and kingship, isolated enough. Nor was individual self-consciousness sufficiently widespread. Human beings were agreed both as to what constituted reality and as to what were the limits of human possibility; and social change—one of our key words to the understanding of the novel—was by no means the problem it became during the nineteenth and twentieth centuries; nor is it accidental that it was during the nineteenth that the novel revealed itself as the most flexible art form for dealing with social change. When the middle class broke the bounds of the feudal synthesis and took its fustian stance, such a literary form was needed, and the novel was the answer. And it is here that the novel assumed the role which makes it so useful today: it thrives on change and social turbulence.

Vaguely, at first, an awareness had grown in men's minds that social reality had cut loose from its traditional base and that new possibilities of experience and new forms of personality had been born into the awfully expanded world. Old class lines were being liquidated and new lines were being formed and broken and re-formed again; new types of men were arising mysteriously out of a whirling social reality which revealed itself protean in its ability to change its appearance and its alignments rapidly, ruthless in its impiety toward old images of order, toward traditional modes of behavior. This is of course to telescope many things; there were several phases of the novel and many variations on the form—from the picaresque to the more stable and refined novel of manners, from the sociology-obsessed novel to the Flaubertian "art" novel —nevertheless, the form attempted to deal with the disparate experiences which society now threw up, and it tried to synthesize these disparate elements. Often quite consciously, and by way of being sheer narrative entertainment, it created new values and affirmed those values which endured specific social changes; and it rejected those acts and ideals which threatened middle-class society.

Perhaps the novel evolved in order to deal with man's growing awareness that behind the façade of social organization, manners, customs, myths, rituals, religions of the post-Christian era, lies chaos. Man knows, despite the certainties which it is the psycho-logical function of his social institutions to give him, that he did not create the universe and that the universe is not at all concerned with human values. Man knows even in this day of marvelous technology and the tenuous subjugation of the atom, that nature can crush him, and that at the boundaries of human order the arts and the instruments of technology are hardly more than magic objects which serve to aid us in our ceaseless quest for certainty. We cannot live, as someone has said, in the contempla-tion of chaos, but neither can we live without an awareness of chaos, and the mean through which we achieve that awareness, and through which we assert our humanity most significantly against it, is great art. And in our time the most articulate art form for defining ourselves and for asserting our humanity is the novel. Certainly it is our most rational art form for dealing with the irrational.

In the nineteenth century, during the moment of greatest middle-class stability—a stability found actually only at the center and there only relatively, in England and not in the colonies; in Paris rather than in Africa, for there the baser instincts, the violence and greed could destroy and exploit non-European societies in the name of humanism and culture, beauty and liberty, fraternity and equality while protecting the humanity of those at home—the novel reached its first high point of formal self-consciousness. Appropriated by the middle class (for such art forms are the creation of total civilizations, not of a single class), it was characterized by an expansiveness which reflected a class of people who had learned to live with the tempo of change and to absorb the effects of change into its frame of existence. And it marked the course of its development and charted the health of its ideals. Perhaps we admire the nineteenth century European novel today, in our time of frantic uncertainty, because we find it vibrant and alive and confidently able to confront good and evil in all their contradictory entanglement. In it was implicit the tragic realization that the treasure of possibility is always to be found in the cave of chaos, guarded by the demons of destruction. It is Abel Magwitch, the jailbird, who makes Pip's dream of a gentleman's life a reality in *Great Expectations*; just as it was the existence of human slavery and colonial exploitation which made possible many of the brighter achievements of modern civilization. And just as the muted insincerities and snobberies of Jane Austen's characters are but highly refined versions of those major insincerities and snobberies, connected with the exercise of power, which have led in our time to the steady crumbling of the empire upon which genteel English society has rested. In that moment of genteel stability, however, those who were most willfully aware of their destiny viewed freedom not simply in terms of necessity but in terms of possibility, and they were willing to take the risks necessary to attain their goals. It was the novel which could communicate their awareness of this sense of possibility along with its cost, and it was the novel which could, on the other hand, reconstruct an image of experience which would make it unnecessary for one to be aware of the true reality upon which society rested. Men, it is said, can stand reality in small doses only, and the novel, sometimes consciously, sometimes not, measured out that dosage.

This was the dark side of the novel's ability to forge images which would strengthen man's will to say No to chaos and affirm him in his task of humanizing himself and the world. It would, even while "entertaining" him, help create that fragile state of human certainty and stability (or the illusion of it at least, for perhaps illusion is all we ever have) and communion which is sometimes called love, brotherhood, democracy, sometimes simply the good life! And it could limit those who would share that life and justify our rejection of their humanity and, while condemning snobbery, could yet condone it, for society was admittedly hieratic and closed to pressure from below.

Enough of general definition; if the novel had not existed at the time the United States started becoming conscious of itself as a nation—a process still, fortunately, for ourselves and the world, unachieved—it would have been necessary for Americans to invent it. For in no other country was change such a given factor of existence; in no other country were the class lines so fluid and change so swift and continuous *and intentional*. In no other country were men so conscious of having defined their social aims nor so committed to working toward making that definition a reality. Indeed, a conscious awareness of values describes the condition of the American experiment, and very often much of our energy goes into finding ways of losing that consciousness. In the beginning was not only the word but its contradiction.

I would be on dangerous ground if I tried to trace too closely a connection between documents of state and literature, since in literature universality is an accepted aim; yet the novel is an art of the specific, and for my own working orientation that connection exists in the United States beyond all questions of cultural chauvinism. Certainly this is evident in our great nineteenth century novels. The moral imperatives of American life that are implicit in the Declaration of Independence, the Constitution, and the Bill of Rights were a part of both the individual consciousness and the conscience of those writers who created what we consider our classic novels—Hawthorne, Melville, James, and Twain; and for all the hooky-playing attitude of the twenties or the political rebelliousness of the thirties, and the reluctance of contemporary writers to deal explicitly with politics, they still are. They are in fact the baffle against which Mr. Lionel Trilling's "hum and buzz of implication" (his understandably vague definition of manners in the novel) sound. These documents form the ground of assumptions upon which our social values rest; they inform our language and our conduct with public meaning, and they provide the broadest frame of reference for our most private dramas. One might deliberately overemphasize and say that most prose fiction in the United States—even the most banal bedroom farce, or the most rarefied, stylized, and understated comedy of manners—is basically "about" the values and cost of living in a democracy. Being an American, wrote Henry James, is a complex fate, but perhaps far more troublesome than the necessity of guarding against superstitious overevaluation of Europe is the problem of dealing with the explicitness of the omnipresent American ideal. For out of the consciously experimental and revolutionary origins of the country has grown the obsession with defining the American experience; first in order to distinguish it from that of Europe and now to determine our uniqueness as a civilization and our proper historical role among the nations. The impetus was twofold, the need to achieve national self-consciousness being, from the beginning, a political goal springing from our rejection of European social forms; and along with this was the pressure of our broad cultural diversification brought about by the open character of the society, the waves of immigration and the rapid expansion, horizontally along the frontier and then vertically through the processes of urbanization and industrialization. Out of this came our most urgent problem of identity, and who and what is American are still perplexing questions even today. Many definitions are offered, in naturalistic art, in *Life* picture portfolios of the American woman, in government photographs of American workers (in which one seldom sees a Negro), in the racial and aesthetic types of movie queens, in works of sociology, in attempts to depict aspects of the American experience in novels—but few are acceptable without qualification, not even during wartime. All Americans are in this sense members of minority groups, even the Anglo-Saxons, whose image has from the beginning dominated all the rest—and one meaning of the social friction in American life is the struggle of each racial, cultural, and religious group to have its own contribution to the national image recognized and accepted. The novelist can bemoan this pressure, for it can be oppressive, but he cannot escape it; and indeed, in our time, it might be his road to a meaningful relationship to the community. "Who," asks Constance Rourke in her *American Humor*, "ever heard of a significant English novel called *The Englishman*, or an excellent French novel called *Le*

Français? The simple aggressive stress belonged to an imagination perennially engaged by the problem of the national type. . . ."

Moreover, this national need gives us a clue to one of the enduring functions of the American novel, which is that of defining the national type as it evolves in the turbulence of change, and of giving the American experience, as it unfolds in its diverse parts and regions, imaginative integration and moral continuity. Thus it is bound up with our problem of nationhood. During the nineteenth century it was clearly recognized by those writers who speak meaningfully to us today, and it comes through novels which in their own times went, like *Moby Dick*, unread. *Moby Dick, The Adventures of Huckleberry Finn, The Bostonians*, and so on, are all "regional" novels, and each simultaneously projects an image of a specific phase of American life, and each is concerned with the moral predicament of the nation. For all the optimism of the early years, there was in this literature no easy affirmation, and for all its involvement with a common set of political and social assumptions, there was, as the list makes plain, no lack of variety of theme. It has been observed that modern American fiction is the only body of literature which is not the work of intellectuals, yet from the beginning our novelists have been consciously concerned with the form, technique, and content of the novel, not excluding ideas. What the observer (a Frenchman) missed was that the major ideas of our society were so alive in the minds of every reader that they could be stated implicitly in the contours of the form. For it is all grounded in a body of the most abstract and explicitly stated conceptions of human society and one which in the form of the great documents of state constitutes a body of assumptions about human possibility which is shared by all Americans—even those who resist most violently any attempt to embody them in social action.

Indeed, these assumptions have been questioned and resisted

from the very beginning, for man cannot simply say, "Let us have liberty and justice and equality for all," and have it; and a democracy more than any other system is always pregnant with its contradiction. The contradiction was to erupt in the Civil War, an event which has had a profound effect upon the direction of our fiction and which continues to influence our thinking about the novel far more than we bother to recognize. For it marked an interruption of our moral continuity, and the form of our novels changed as a result.

As Henry James wrote in his study of Hawthorne:

The subsidence of that great convulsion has left a different tone from the tone it found, and one may say that the Civil War marks an era in the history of the American mind. It introduced into the national consciousness a certain sense of proportion and relation, of the world being a more complicated place than it had hitherto seemed, the future more treacherous, success more difficult. At the rate at which things are going, it is obvious that good Americans will be more numerous than ever; but the good American, in days to come, will be a more critical person than his complacent and confident grandfather. He has eaten of the tree of knowledge. He will not, I think, be a sceptic, and still less, of course, a cynic; but he will be, without discredit to his well-known capacity for action, an observer. He will remember that the ways of the Lord are inscrutable, and that this is a world in which everything happens; and eventualities, as the late Emperor of the French used to say, will not find him intellectually unprepared.

Actually the good American fell quite a bit short of James's prediction, and he made far less of his traumatic fraternal conflict than might have been expected. And if it did not make him skeptical (and how could he have been really, with all the material progress released after the war with which to affirm his optimism?), it did make him evasive and given to compromise on basic principles. As a result we have the interruption of moral

70

continuity symbolized in the failure of Reconstruction and the Hayes-Tilden Compromise, and now in the 1950's, at a time when our world leadership has become an indisputable and perplexing fact, we have been forced to return to problems, in the form of the current desegregation issue, which should have been faced up to years ago. What is more, the event of World War I found the good American hardly less innocent than he had been fifty-three years before; only now, instead of such critical and morally affirmative novels as *Huckleberry Finn, The Gilded Age,* or *The Bostonians* (in which James depicts the decay of moral values among those who had been leaders in the struggle for abolition) or *Moby Dick* or *The Confidence-Man,* we had literature which came out of the individual writer's private need to express a national mood of glamourized social irresponsibility. Certainly the attitude of moral evasion expressed in the failure of Reconstruction and the materialism of the Gilded Age prepared for the mood of glamourized social irresponsibility voiced in the fiction of the twenties, and it created a special problem between the American novelist and his audience.

Being committed to optimism, serious novels have always been troublesome to Americans, precisely because of their involvement with our problem of identity. If they depict too much of reality they frighten us by giving us a picture of society frozen at a point so far from our optimistic ideal (for in depiction there is a freezing as well as a discovery and release of possibility) that we feel compelled to deny it. Yet if they leave out too much we cannot take them seriously for very long, even though we might buy them in hundreds of thousands of copies. As readers we wait for definition and even now in this so-called age of conformity we wish to discover some transcendent meaning in at least some of the turbulence which whirls through our lives, and which during a period of highest prosperity makes it necessary for all the media of communication to set up an incessant "hard sell" incantation to reassure us that all is well, all meaningful, the very best state of affairs; that things confer happiness, beauty, and grace; and that fertility is a smiling face in a magazine ad.

Another way of putting it is that we are a people who, while desiring identity, have been reluctant to pay the cost of its achievement. We have been reluctant since we first suspected that we are fated to live up to our sacred commitments or die, and the Civil War was the form of that fateful knowledge. Thus we approach serious novels with distrust until the moment comes when the passage of time makes it possible for us to ignore their moral cutting edge. In the nineteenth century serious fiction was fairly easily disposed of—it was given to children, especially to boys; and then only after being purged of those matters that were less likely to disturb the juvenile than his parents. *Huckleberry Finn* was banned from libraries, *Moby Dick* went unread, and those who understood James were very few. It was as though the older generation was saying, "These are problems which you are likely to encounter when you come of age; we are too busy making progress to give them our attention"; but when the younger generation was grown up so much had happened in the swift change, and they had been joined by so many new arrivals, that they forgot both the nature of the problem and its historical source. By the twenties the relationship between the serious novel and themselves as readers had undergone a remarkable change, and if they had lost little of the simplicity of James's earlier good American they were now full of doubts as to the possibility of the ideal and they had begun to resent it much as they resented the necessity of participating in the war.

And so with the novel; where before it had affirmed the sacred assumptions, now, as in the Caporetto scene in *A Farewell to Arms*, it denied the very words in which the ideals were set down. The nineteenth century novelist had stood within society even as he criticized its behavior, and now the novelist thought of himself as alienated. Yet, ironically, men like Fitzgerald and Hemingway were actually more celebrated than any American writer since Mark Twain. America, for all her shocks and traumas, has been an extremely lucky country, and Time, as with the little boy in Dylan Thomas's poem, has let her be "golden in the mercy of his means," allowing her a generosity of mistakes and laxities and a childlike ability to forget her falls from grace, wealth and movement and a ruddy strength of people and national resources and a ceaseless stream of wonderful toys with which to excite her imagination and to keep her unaware of Time's ambiguousness—and her luck was extended to her writers of the twenties.

After the clangor and pain of the war and its booming echo in the expansion and hysterical faddism of the twenties, the moral irresponsibility had become so chronic that one would have expected the writers either to depict it critically or to become silent, but instead they had the luck to give at least part of their attention to the so-called revolution of the word, which was offered as a literary equivalent of that distraction from the realities of the moral situation provided by the material prosperity of the boom. Nor was it simply a matter of luck. For all their pose of alienation, the writers of the twenties worked hard, found images that were simple enough to project those feelings of impotence and moral irresponsibility that were typical of the times, and make them romantically attractive. The brave lonely man, broken by war and betrayed by politicians, who had lost faith in everything except the basic processes of existence and his own physical strength; who could no longer believe in the old American creed; who traveled to Pamplona and Paris, who drank too much and who made love compulsively and was romantically unhappy (but who yet had the money to indulge in his escape) became the dominant image of the American. And so gripping was this image that some critics look back today and actually confuse the image with the reality of the times.

By the twenties, in other words, the novel, which in the hands of our greatest writers had been a superb moral instrument, became morally diffident and much of its energy was turned upon itself in the form of technical experimentation. Which is not to deny a writer like Hemingway has profound moral seriousness, or to imply that technique is ever void of moral implications, but to say that here the personal despair which gave the technique its resonance became a means of helping other Americans to avoid those aspects of reality which they no longer had the will to face. This is the tragedy implicit in Hemingway's morality of craftsmanship, the attempt to make a highly personal morality the informing motive of an art form which by its very nature is extremely social and, despite its pose, deeply rooted in the assumption it denied. For as I read Hemingway today I find that he affirms the old American values by the eloquence of his denial; makes his moral point by stating explicitly that he does not believe in morality; achieves his eloquence through denying eloquence; and is most moral when he denies the validity of a national morality which the nation has not bothered to live up to since the Civil War. The confusion—for both Hemingway's imitators and his readers—lay in the understatement, and here the basic American assumptions exerted their power. For although it is seldom mentioned, Hemingway is as obsessed with the Civil War and its aftermath as any Southern writer, and the fact turns up constantly in his work. The children of the good Americans of the eighties had forgotten the historical problems which made Hemingway's understatement fully meaningful—even though it was here exactly that the ideas which were said to be absent were most present and powerful. But many readers, unhappy with the compact we'd made with history, took the novelist's point of view as authority to go on a binge of hooky-playing, as an assurance that there were no new lessons to learn and the old ones were invalid anyway. And this with the Depression only a few years away.

Yet so fascinating were the images of the twenties, and so deep and irrational the feelings which they made articulate, that thirty years later critics who readily admit the superficiality of most novels written during the thirties (for they tried to be responsible by avoiding complexity), and who reject most contemporary fiction even when written to their formulas, insist that we measure ourselves by the triumphs of the twenties. They tell us again and again of the Lost Generation novelists, and their names (with Faulkner's recently added) clang in our ears like gongs in evidence of our failure and our doom. They, we are told, did that which we cannot hope to do, and if this fails to discourage us the nineteenth century novel of manners is held before us as final evidence of our futility and the novel's point of highest glory and swift decline.

Not that we disagree absolutely with any of this, but we must reply to these charges. Thank God that we can't do what the Lost Generation novelists did, because as good as it was, it was not good enough nor broad enough to speak for today. And thank God again that the nineteenth century European novel of manners is dead, for it has little value in dealing with our world of chaos and catastrophe. We have lived a different life and we have seen it with different eyes. Nor are we innocent of the world's new complexity or given to false pieties, easy hopes, or facile rejections; nor are we unaware of the weakness implicit in our tremendous strength, or of the possibilities of strength in our apparent weaknesses, for the iron-weight of tragic awareness has descended upon us. Ours is a task which, whether recognized or not, was defined for us to a large extent by that which the novels of the twenties failed to confront, and implicit in their triumphs and follies were our complexity and our travail.

75

Indeed, so much has been written about the triumphs of the twenties that we either forget its failures or forgive them; which would be well if the critics would only leave it at that. But the contemporary novelist cannot afford to forget the failures, even if he makes no accusations, and the intentions of such a novelist as Saul Bellow can be properly understood only in light of that failure. After two well written, neatly constructed novels which paid their respects to the standards of the twenties, Bellow's major work to date is *The Adventures of Augie March*, which at first glance looks like the work of a completely different man. It is characterized by a big conception of human possibility and a quality of wonder arising out of the mysteriousness of a reality which keeps its secret despite the documentation of the social scientists, and it is informed by a knowledge of chaos which would have left the novelists of the twenties discouraged. Certainly it confronts large areas of American reality which simply didn't get into the novels of the twenties.

I would go further here and say that neither the American fiction of the twenties nor that of the fifties can be understood outside the perspective provided by the nineteenth century. Edmund Wilson seems to suggest this by his current reexamination of the Civil War and post-Reconstruction periods, and certainly the younger writers who came through the Depression and who shared the social and political preoccupations of the thirties feel this, even though they've bothered little to write about it. Yet it is one of the goals of the current serious novel to create precisely that moral perspective. Here perhaps is one of our most serious failures, for not only has the drift of our internal social affairs brought this period and its unsolved moral problems back into the national consciousness; world events have revealed their broad relevance to areas far beyond our national borders. In other words, the events which racked the United States during the Civil War period and again during the twenties were the archetype of events which are now sweeping all societies, and our failure to confront them when they arose (for perhaps they could not have been *solved*) has proved not only an impediment to our leadership among the nations but a hindrance to our achievement of national identity.

Perhaps the attitude of those novelists who matured during the forties has been too quietly aloof, our absorption in craft problems too concentrated, and our dependence upon the perceptiveness of critics too trusting. Perhaps we who disdain the easy pose are far more alienated than the writers of the Lost Generation, for we have assumed an understanding on the part of both reader and critic which is at best rare, and we fail to say very much that is explicit about our intentions or points of view.

By contrast the writers of the twenties did a brilliant job of publicizing their own efforts. During the time when *Ulysses* and *Finnegans Wake* were being written, both were being eagerly discussed in several languages and in several countries. Because Joyce (no member of the Lost Generation but the most "difficult" novelist of the period) was not only writing his books; he was, with the help of magazine editors, friends, and critics, just as busily establishing the convention by which he wished his novels read. Whatever his success in absenting himself from his novels as omniscient author—a technical problem already solved by Conrad and James—in his correspondence he did anything but pare his nails; he was far too busy telling those who tell the readers how to read just what the godlike author was about. Clearly it is no accident that more people have read about how his books should be read than have read them. And for all of the legend of Hemingway's nonintellectuality, and the aesthetic ideas spun in metaphors from the sports, he has nevertheless written so much and so significantly about writing that two younger writers are busy making a volume of his observations. One needs but mention the examples of Eliot, Gertrude Stein, Ezra Pound, and Henry James before them.

Looked at coldly, the notion of a Lost Generation was a literary conceit of such major proportions that today it seems like a swindle. The alienation of these writers had something of the character of putting on a mask in Macy's window at high noon and pretending that no one knows who you are. They had not only the comfort of being in the well advertised advanced guard; they were widely read and their characters' way of life was imitated to the extent that several generations of young people stylized their speech and attitudes to the pattern of Fitzgerald's and Hemingway's fiction. While "Papa" Hemingway (who *is* the "father" of many writers who today sneer at him) was so alienated that a song, "Pul-eeze, Mr. Hemingway," could find popularity. With *Esquire* carrying their work to readers in most of the barbershops throughout the country, these writers were lost in a crowd of admirers, of whom I was one.

For all the personal despair which informed it and the hard work which brought it into being, the emphasis on technique gave something of a crossword-puzzle-fad aspect to the literature of the twenties, and very often the question of the Sphinx was lost in the conundrums. Without doubt, major questions went unanswered. Yet happily its concentration upon the problems of craft made it impossible for us to ignore the fact that literature, to the extent that it is art, is *artificial*. Each of us must learn to read and to understand the devices through which fiction achieves its illusion of reality. Thanks to their popularizers and the generations of critics who followed, we know how to read their books extremely well—especially in terms of those matters which preoccupied them—and the level of craft consciousness is so high in the United States that today by keeping to formula and the neat theme (neat because smoothed down and polished since Flaubert's time) the writer may turn out readable, smoothly fashioned novels which evoke a response much like that we extend those miniaturists who work in ivory. The phrases are neatly done, there is a great economy of means (because so little of substance) and tightness of structure, great texture and facile sensibility; and anyone who has had a course in modern literature or who has read a little criticism has the satisfaction of knowing just how each image and metaphor operates, who the hero's literary ancestors were, just how Joyce, James, Freud, Marx, Sartre, Camus, Unamuno, Kierkegaard, and Fitzgerald, Hemingway, and Lionel Trilling, came into it. There is, in this writing, no excess of emotion (if any at all) nor shrillness of tone; no vulgarity nor uncertainties of taste; nor are there any patterns of action that would violate the assumptions concerning life or art that are held by the most timid middle-class reader. The writer may, if he likes, play the turns of the whole corpus of genteel nineteenth and twentieth century fiction, especially the European, and never exhaust himself in the process of translating these well polished themes and situations into American backgrounds, and utilizing along the way all the latest verbal techniques approved by the critics.

Despite their skill, however, these novels are not widely read, and the reader who looks here for some acknowledgment of the turbulence he feels around him would be better satisfied by a set of comic books. He thus turns to "fact" books for "scientific" consolation because the orientation in reality which the novel should afford him is not forthcoming, and the critics, appalled by the stillborn children which they have called forth, look backward to those highly dubious Edens of the nineteenth century and of the Lost Generation, and pronounce the novel dead. If so, perhaps they have helped to dig its grave.

For if the nineteenth century way with troublesome novels was to turn them over to the children, we in our time, being more sophisticated and literate, turn them over to the critics, who proceed to reduce the annoying elements to a minimum. And more deplorable is that fact that once the critics have spoken, the story is likely to appear in subsequent editions with the troublesome, the difficult material, edited out—as happened to one of the most sublime stories in the language—really an extremely foreshortened novel—Faulkner's "The Bear." Perhaps the test of a work's becoming a classic in the United States depends upon the extent to which it can withstand this process of conscious reduction. Perhaps what I am saying is that since the novel is a moral instrument possessing for us an integrative function, our typical American reaction to it is to evade so much of its moral truth as possible; perhaps out of an effort to postpone completing that identity which we are compelled nonetheless to seek. But as to the critics' role in this process, I am struck that while their reductions are made on aesthetic grounds, it turns out that what they consider expendable is usually the heart of the fiction. And here, out of fairness I must include novelists like James and Hemingway who, by way of defining their own aesthetic positions, have contributed to some of the current confusion.

Let us take Henry James on Hawthorne, Hemingway on *The Adventures of Huckleberry Finn,* and Malcolm Cowley on Faulkner's "The Bear." These three, because each has been quite influential in shaping our ideas of American fiction and how it should be read and because at least two have been offered as guides for the younger novelists who have come upon the scene since the thirties. Each of the texts constitutes a definition of American fiction; each has been most helpful in giving us orientation, and today all three have become quite mischievous in adding to the current confusion over the role, the character, and the condition of the contemporary novel. Indeed, it is as though a set of familiar and useful touchstones had become inflated and transformed into a set of wandering rocks which threatens to crush us.

Each of the texts which I shall quote is so familiar that there would be no need to quote them except for the fact that each has achieved its importance by virtue of its being a statement by reduction of either a perceptive critical observation or the meaning of an important novel. So that in order to determine where we are and how we arrived at some of our current convictions concerning the novel it is useful to take a look at exactly what was discarded from the originals.

Mr. Trilling has almost alone been responsible for making a single statement of Henry James more prominent in our thinking than all the complex aesthetic ideas spelled out in the Prefaces and the essays. In developing his theory of the novel of manners, he paraphrases James's catalogue of those items of civilization which were missing from Hawthorne's America, itself an extension of a list which Hawthorne had himself made in the preface to his novel *Transformation* (*The Marble Faun*):

No author, without a trial, can conceive of the difficulty of writing a romance about a country where there is no shadow, no antiquity, no mystery, no picturesque and gloomy wrong, nor anything but a commonplace prosperity, in broad and simple daylight, as is happily the case with my dear native land.

This is Mr. Hawthorne, and while admiring what he made of his position one must observe that in this world one finds that which one has the eyes to see. Certainly there was gloomy wrong enough both in the crime against the Indians and in the Peculiar Institution which was shortly to throw the country into conflict; there was enough mystery in Abraham Lincoln's emergence, then in process, still to excite us with wonder; and in that prosperity and "broad and simple daylight" enough evil was brewing to confound us even today. But let us see what James made of this quote, for it is upon James that Mr. Trilling bases much of his argument:

The perusal of Hawthorne's American Note-Books operates as a practical commentary upon this somewhat ominous text. It does so at least to my own mind; it would be too much perhaps to say that the effect would be the same for the usual English reader. An American reads between the lines—he completes the suggestions—he constructs a picture. I think I am not guilty of any gross injustice in saying that the picture he constructs from Hawthorne's American diaries, though by no means without charms of its own, is not, on the whole, an interesting one. It is characterized by an extraordinary blankness—a curious paleness of colour and paucity of detail. Hawthorne, as I have said, has a large and healthy appetite for detail, and one is therefore the more struck with the lightness of the diet to which his observation was condemned. For myself, as I turn the pages of his journals, I seem to see the image of the crude and simple society in which he lived. I use these epithets, of course, not invidiously, but descriptively; if one desire to enter as closely as possible into Hawthorne's situation, one must endeavour to reproduce his circumstances. We are struck with the large number of elements that were absent from them, and the coldness, the thinness, the blankness, to repeat my epithet, present themselves so vividly that our foremost feeling is that of compassion for a romancer looking for subjects in such a field. It takes so many things, as Hawthorne must have felt later in life, when he made the acquaintance of the denser, richer, warmer European spectacle—it takes such an accumulation of history and custom, such a complexity of manners and types, to form a fund of suggestion for a novelist. If Hawthorne had been a young Englishman, or a young Frenchman of the same degree of genius, the same cast of mind, the same habits, his consciousness of the world around him would have been a very different affair; however obscure, however reserved, his own personal life, his sense of the life of his fellow-mortals would have been almost infinitely more various. The negative side of the spectacle on which Hawthorne looked out, in his contemplative saunterings and reveries, might, indeed [And it is here that Mr. Trilling's much repeated paraphrase begins], with a little ingenuity, be made almost ludicrous; one might enumerate the items of high civilization, as it exists in other countries, which are absent from the texture of American life, until it should become a wonder to know what was left. No State, in the European sense of the word, and indeed barely a specific national name. No sovereign, no court, no personal loyalty, no aristocracy,

no church, no clergy, no army, no diplomatic service, no country
gentlemen, no palaces, nor castles, nor manors, nor old country-houses,
nor parsonages, nor thatched cottages, nor ivied ruins; no cathedrals,
nor abbeys, nor little Norman churches; no great Universities nor
public schools—no Oxford, nor Eton, nor Harrow; no literature, no
novels, no museums, no pictures, no political society, no sporting class
—no Epsom nor Ascot! Some such list as that might be drawn up
of the absent things in American life—especially in the American
life of forty years ago, the effect of which, upon an English or a
French imagination, would probably as a general thing be appalling.
The natural remark, in the almost lurid light of such an indictment,
would be that if these things are left out, everything is left out. [And
it is here that Mr. Trilling leaves us.] The American knows that a
good deal remains; what it is that remains—that is his secret, his joke,
as one may say. It would be cruel, in this terrible denudation, to
deny him the consolation of his natural gift, that "American humour"
of which of late years we have heard so much.

"That is," says Mr. Trilling, "no sufficiency of means for the
display of a variety of manners, no opportunity for the novelist
to do his job of searching out reality, not enough complication
of appearance to make the job interesting." Mr. Trilling states
in the same essay that while we have had great novels in America,
they "diverge from [the novel's] classic intention . . . the investi-
gation of the problem of reality beginning in the social field."

All this is admittedly a damaging list—of reasons why American novelists cannot write French or English novels of manners.
And when I read the much quoted passage in context (one of
Mr. Trilling's disciples has deduced from it that personality exists
in the United States only in New England and in the South) it
struck me as amusing that Mr. Trilling missed the point that
these lacks were seen as appalling for the French or English
imagination—for it seems obvious that in that time neither
Frenchmen nor Englishmen were going to try to write American
novels (though things are different today), that James was
addressing his remarks to Europeans and that all the energy that

has been wasted in bemoaning the fact that American society is not English or French society could have stopped right there.

James's remarks on Hawthorne are justified to the extent that the perspective he was creating helped him to establish his own point of departure; it is to the insistence that his observations be binding upon other writers that I object. Nor can I overlook the fact that James was basing his remarks on the thinness of Hawthorne's notebooks—which, compared with James's, were thin indeed. Yet just when, one might ask without too much irreverence, did a writer's quality—James's prolific notebooks notwithstanding—depend upon the kind of notebooks he kept? Did anyone ever see Shakespeare's notebooks? And would anyone who read Dostoevski's *A Writer's Diary* without an acquaintance with the novels suspect that it was the journal of one of the greatest novelists of all time?

For me the most surprising aspect of Mr. Trilling's paraphrase is that he says nothing at all concerning what James calls the "American joke"—a matter which, as a novelist, intrigues me no end. I take it that James's reference to American humor was nothing more than condescension and that he did not mean it in the sense that it was used by Miss Constance Rourke, who saw American humor as having the function of defining and consolidating the diverse elements—racial, cultural, and otherwise—which go into the American character; a business to which James made a profound contribution, even when irritated by what he considered the thinness of American experience. One wonders what the state of novel criticism would be today if Mr. Trilling had turned his critical talent to an examination of the American joke. Perhaps *this* has been the objective of the American novel all along, even the Jamesian novel, and perhaps this is its road to health even today.

But now another touchstone: "All modern American literature comes from one book by Mark Twain called *Huckleberry Finn*

. . . it's the best book we've had. All American writing comes from that." So wrote Ernest Hemingway in *Green Hills of Africa* in a much quoted statement. It is significant that here again we have a statement by reduction which, although it helped Hemingway to create his own position, has helped us ignore what seems to me to be the very heart of *Huckleberry Finn.* He tells us in the same context that we should stop reading at the point where Nigger Jim is stolen from Huck and Tom Sawyer because from that point on it is cheating. And here we have something different from the first example and perhaps, in light of Hemingway's great influence upon American fiction, more important. In order to define his own position (or perhaps to justify it, since the statement comes some ten years after he caught the public's imagination) Hemingway found it necessary to reduce the meaning of *Huckleberry Finn* to the proportions of his own philosophical position. Far more meaningful to him than the moral vision and sense of language which summoned them into being were the techniques through which Twain gave it expression. And so with the critics who usually quote Hemingway's remarks with the most important phrase in his statement omitted. For when he goes on to advise us that we should stop reading *Huckleberry Finn* at that point where Nigger Jim is stolen from Huck and Tom Sawyer, he reveals either a blindness to the moral point of the novel or his own inability to believe in the moral necessity which makes Huck know that he must *at least make the attempt* to get Jim free; to "steal" him free, is the term by which Twain reveals Huck's full awareness of the ambiguousness of his position, and through which he roots the problem in American social reality and draws upon the contradiction between democratic idealism and the existence of slavery. Nevertheless, it is exactly that part of the action which represents the formal externalization of Huck-Twain's moral position; and if one may speak of ritual here, it is in this part of the action that the fundamental American commitment, the myth, is made manifest. Without this attempt *Huckleberry Finn* becomes the simple boy's book that many would rather it be, a fantasy born of pure delight and not really serious at all.

Yet Hemingway is a most serious author and in this statement he not only tells us more about himself than about Twain or American fiction, he expresses the basic difference in points of view between nineteenth and twentieth century writers. Thus not only did *Huckleberry Finn* lose some of its meaning; many of those whom it might have helped to some sense of the moral and historical continuity of American life were advised, in effect, that such continuity was nonexistent. But it is useless to quarrel with history, and as one who is committed to the craft I can even admit that Hemingway's art justifies what he made of Twain's. But what are we to say of the critics who circulate his statement as though it were the word of God? What of their responsibility to the reader?

One can easily agree with Hemingway as to the importance of *Huckleberry Finn* in the continuity of the American novel while rejecting his dismissal of its ethical intention, for we have in William Faulkner a twentieth century writer who not only continues, in his own way, the technical direction outlined by Mark Twain but also, despite Lionel Trilling's dismissal of him as "being limited to a provincial scene," continues the moral commitment which was at the heart of Twain's fiction.

Just as experimental and technically "difficult" as Hemingway and, perhaps, as Joyce, Faulkner missed the broad publicity accorded their experimentation; not only because his more important works were published somewhat later, but because there is no doubt that he is involved both as a Southerner and as an artist with those issues which most white Americans have evaded since the Civil War. Thus it was not until about 1946 that Faulkner began to win the attention of Americans generally,

and a great aid in this was the Viking Portable, edited by Malcolm Cowley. By this time several of the most important novels
were out of print, and one cannot overstress the service rendered
by Cowley and the publisher in issuing their collection with
Cowley's introduction and commentary. Through it many Americans not only made their first contact with a great writer but
were introduced to a superb imaginative account of what so
much of the conflict in American life is all about. Thus my reason
for mentioning Cowley's reduction of the meaning of Faulkner's
"The Bear" is not to detract from the importance of the Portable, but further to illustrate the reduction of the moral intention
of American prose fiction by way of making it easier for the
reader.

"The Bear" [writes Mr. Cowley] is the longest of Faulkner's stories
and in many ways the best. It is divided into five parts. If you want to
read simply a hunting story, and one of the greatest in the language,
you should confine yourself to the first three parts and the last, which
are written in Faulkner's simplest style. The long fourth part is harder
to read and deals with more complicated matters. In it Faulkner
carries to an extreme his effort toward putting the whole world into
one sentence, between one capital letter and one period. . . . In all this
section of "The Bear" the reader may have difficulty in fitting the
subjects to the predicates and in disentangling the subordinate clauses;
and yet, if he perseveres, he will discover one of Faulkner's most im-
pressive themes: the belief in Isaac McCaslin's heart that the land itself
had been cursed by slavery, and that the only way for him to escape
the curse was to relinquish the land.

But not only does this fourth section (which takes up thirty-
four of the 136 pages) contain this theme; it is in fact the dis-
located beginning of the story and the time-present in which the
bear hunt is evoked out of the memory of the hero who, at the
age of twenty-one, confronts his cousin with his decision to give
up the land. Although it has recently been included in a volume

of hunting stories with the fourth section missing, "The Bear" is not about a bear hunt at all, but about a young American's hunt for moral identity. Significantly, it is the centerpiece of a volume which takes its title from the Negro spiritual "Go Down, Moses," and its main concern is with the problem of American freedom as faced by a specific white Southerner in relation to his individual heritage. Here, in *Go Down Moses*, Faulkner comes most passionately to grips with the moral implications of slavery, the American land, progress and materialism, tradition and moral identity—all major themes of the American novel. And it is in the fourth section—not really difficult once it is grasped that it is a remembered dialogue with the "he saids" left out—where Isaac and his cousin McCaslin argue out the issues between them (McCaslin basing his arguments on tradition and history and Isaac on a form of Christian humanism), that Faulkner makes his most extended effort to define the specific form of the American Negro's humanity and to get at the human values which were lost by both North and South during the Civil War. Even more important, it is here that Isaac McCaslin demonstrates one way in which the individual American can assert his freedom from the bonds of history, tradition, and things, and thus achieve moral identity. Whether we accept Isaac McCaslin's solution or not, the problem is nevertheless basic to democratic man—as it was to Ahab and as it was to Huck Finn.

Nor do I wish to oversimplify Mr. Cowley's problem; if serious fiction is to be made available to those to whom it is addressed, those who, as Ike McCaslin puts it, "have nothing else to read with but the heart," the critic must interpret for them and in the process of making literature available to all the levels of a democratic society some loss of quality, some blunting of impact, seems inevitable. Nevertheless the critic has some responsibility in seeing that the reader does not evade the crucial part of a fiction simply because of its difficulty. For sometimes the diffi-

culty is the mark of the writer's deepest commitment to life and
to his art. To water down his work is not only to mock the
agony and the joy which go into his creation but to rob the reader
of that transcendence which, despite his tendency to evade the
tragic aspects of reality, he seeks in literature. The intent of
criticism is frustrated, the fiction reduced to mere entertainment,
and the reader is encouraged to evade self-scrutiny. In the leveling
process to which all things are subjected in a democracy one must
depend always upon the *individual's* ability to rise out of the
mass and achieve the possibility implicit in the society. One
must depend upon his ability, whoever he is and from whatever
class and racial group, to attain the finest perception of human
value, to become as consciously aware of life, say, as any of
Henry James's "super-subtle fry." Certainly the novelist must
make some such assumption if he is to allow himself range in
which to work toward the finest possibilities of his talent and his
form without a frustrating sense of alienation.

Which tells us something of why the novelists keep writing
despite the current attempts to legislate the novel a quiet death.
It also gives us a hint as to why a number of the younger novelists
are not at all hindered by the attempt to reduce the novel to only
one of its possible forms; yes, and why the picaresque, many-
leveled novel, swarming with characters and with varied types
and levels of experience, has appeared among us. Though we love
the classics, some of us have little interest in what Mr. Trilling
calls the "novel of manners," and I don't believe that a society
hot in the process of defining itself can for long find its image
in so limited a form. Surely the novel is more than he would have
it be, and if it isn't then we must make it so.

One of the comic aspects to the current controversy over what
a novel should be is the implicit assumption, held by Cooper,
James, and Hawthorne, as well as several contemporary critics,
that society was created mainly so that novelists could write about

it. It is felt that society should be of such shape that the novelist can settle it neatly into prefabricated molds with the least spilling of rude life over the sides. The notion started when the forest was still being cleared, and it is understandable that a certain type of writer would have liked to deal with fine cabinetry instead of crude logs. Still, minds that were philosophically and politically most advanced and sophisticated conceived this society, but even they had nonetheless to deal with raw and rapidly moving materials. And so in the beginning did the American novel, and so today. We are not so crude now as during James's time but we have even less stability and there is no longer a stable England to which to withdraw for perspective. World War I, the Depression, World War II and Korea, the Cold War, the threat of the atom, our discovery of the reality of treason, and now Egypt and Hungary make us aware that reality, which during Dickens's time seemed fairly stable, has broken loose from its old historical base, and the Age of Anxiety is truly more than a poetic conceit. Closed societies are now the flimsy illusions, for all the outsiders are demanding in.

In fact there is no stability anywhere and there will not be for many years to come, and progress now insistently asserts its tragic side; the evil now stares out of the bright sunlight. New groups will ceaselessly emerge, class lines will continue to waver and break and re-form; great wealth there will be and a broader distribution of that wealth, and a broader distribution of ideas along with it. But the problem of what to do with the increased leisure which wealth makes possible will continue to plague us —as will the problem of deciding just what constitutes a truly human way of life. The fundamental problems of the American situation will repeat themselves again and again and will be faced more or less by peoples throughout the world: Where shall we draw the line upon our own freedom in a world in which culture, tradition, and even history have been shaken up? At how fast a pace should we move toward social ideals? What is worth having and what worth holding? Where and in what pattern of conduct does true value, at a given moment, lie? These questions will continue to press upon us even if the dream of world peace is achieved, for they are questions built into the core of modern experience.

For the novelist the existence of these questions creates a basic problem of rhetoric. How does one in the novel (the novel which is a work of art and not a disguised piece of sociology) persuade the American reader to identify that which is basic in man beyond all differences of class, race, wealth, or formal education? How does one not only make the illiterate and inarticulate eloquent enough so that the educated and more favorably situated will recognize wisdom and honor and charity, heroism and capacity for love when found in humble speech and dress? And conversely, how does one persuade readers with least knowledge of literature to recognize the broader values implicit in their lives? How, in a word, do we affirm that which *is* stable in human life beyond and despite all processes of social change? How give the reader that which we do have in abundance, all the countless untold and wonderful variations on the themes of identity and freedom and necessity, love and death, and with all the mystery of personality undergoing its endless metamorphosis?

Here are questions which cannot be answered by criticism; they call for the novel, many novels; and as long as there are writers willing to accept the challenge of reducing the reality in which they exist to living form there will be readers interested in their answers, and we need have no fear that the novel is moribund.

Herbert Gold

The Mystery of Personality in the Novel

THE NOVELIST'S boldest address to himself says: "I must master the most powerful sense of human life on earth, that of individual striving in a world clotted with both trouble and joy; I mean to commit myself to love and ambition and the frustrating of mortality."

The timorous wee clerk within replies, "Who, *you?*"

"Yes," says the novelist, "and don't interrupt. I will reflect the movement of men in society in order to give an example of the glory of desire."

The inner clerk, snuffling righteously before so much rhetoric, says: "Watch out! That's very difficult."

And so it is. And so ensues a struggle. Generally the clerk wins. Often the dialogue is never quite argued through. Occasionally, a few times in each generation, the novelist wins against his other self.

In the first case there is the sleek and pure pseudonovelist, faking passion, faking life, the opportunist of problems, the Herman Wouks and Sloan Wilsons and Cameron Hawleys, with their deep affirmations for those who admire the editorials in *Life*. In the second case there is an uneasy, unfulfilled writer, often precious, satisfied with aspects and insights and partial comfort. And in the third case, when the novelist never abandons his deepest hopes, well, there is the possibility of a masterpiece. He gives us the stories for which we hunger, rich with people we love in mortal danger; his way of telling, his angle of vision, his perspective—this is what we mean by style—gives us the judgment married to perception which defines both the whole man and the artist. Sensitive and brave at the same time—what a monster!—he joins plot and perspective in a way that finally, without exhortation, suggests a vision of the good life.

This is the critical maximum which no individual can reach.

But although it is more pleasant to talk of success, I should like first to name some of the ways by which novelists evade the possibilities of their art. They construct a mannered style of arbitrary perspectives, with the intention that neither they nor their readers will be obliged to venture into the huge mystery of personality. The aim is simple: If you restrict your world, then the world is reduced in size and manageable. Hide what is difficult; trim what does not fit; take it neat. The great novelist is committed to a world without horizons, manifested first of all by a large and lyric sense for his heroes. The mediocre or tertiary writer limits and limits and limits, and so we have, sometimes overlapping, the following contemporary types:

The Forthright Brutes: Ernest Hemingway and imitators. They are bewitched boys, newly discovering verbs and nouns, physical sensation, zip-pow-wham of weather, drink, sex, war, bulls. They are too scared of what goes on inside an intelligence, inside a memory, inside a group of people to be able to face these matters except by smashing physical symbols like fists across the page. Sometimes they have sensitive nerves in their fists, but the nerve endings are stunned before making contact with the complex congeries of will and desire within.

Hemingway's resolution of the necessary tension of conception in fiction can be examined in the light of the traditional philosophical concept of universals and particulars. In one tradition "reality" is defined by abstract forms outside time, and the specific ever-changing events of our world are flickering shadows through fire on the wall of the cave, imperfect imitations of the ideal forms. In the other tradition, it is these particular events which are "real," and general statements are inaccurate, merely useful summaries of the only knowable reality—the fact in the here and now. The terms "idealism" and "materialism" are approximate, somewhat misleading labels for these opposing world views.

The novel as a form is obviously empirical, working toward whatever large statements it has to offer about men in society, love, death, ambition, and so on, through specific instances of *a* man, *a* love, *a* death, *an* ambition, a specific society in a specific time and place. Not merely in general approach, but in method also the novelist tends to be empirical. He does not say, "She was beautiful." He describes a particular lovely creature with all her lovely attachments and gadgets, and then leaves us with one of the formal summaries which are part of the reader's active participation in a fiction: "Wow! Beautiful!" The novelist seeks what T. S. Eliot has called, in a famous phrase, the "objective correlative" of emotion.

This objectifying in Hemingway goes very far. It is as if he were a too literal student of some early physical scientist, overskeptical about what he can learn. The abstention from analysis, deduction, conjecture, the bold hunch—these risks which are taken by the great scientist, too—in favor of a minute noting of symptoms has a certain animal simplicity, grace, and power. But even the most graceful and powerful bull hangs from a very small head, which he uses mainly for battering, and little of what one bull learns needs to be passed on to another. He has opted for a pathetic lowering of the eyes, a doomed charge, a sword in the heart, and an occasional chance to gore before thumping in the dust with his life running out. *El pobre toro!* His head admits not enough to understanding.

A passion for objectifying emotion through physical sensation and act spins off to mania in the lesser work of Hemingway and in his fleas. The details become more and more ritual; the general emotion and sense which is supposed to emerge from the details has to be supplied entirely by the reader. In its own way, this is a highly "literary" manner, depending on knowledge of other stories, other stages in the life of the maestro, rather than on the work at hand itself: "It was hot. He took a cigarette. It was very hot. He took a drink. He went upstairs. Christ, it was hot."

This type of minimal statement in Hemingway goes very far toward forgetting that thoughts, fantasies, memories, projects, the constant inner monologue and the unspoken conversations among people are also facts in the world, facts of being human. That we think defines our humanity. We are remembering, reasoning, political creatures, constantly responding to others and constantly willing ourselves into relation with others. Eliminate these actions in the guise of objective reporting and the writer eliminates the properly human, just as at the opposite extreme, in the precious and private writer, he eliminates social meaning by signifying nothing but his own obsession. The force of an obsession cannot be communicated; the obsessed person clings to his loneliness. Hemingway's compulsion toward objectivity links him with the obsessively subjective writer: they both fail to give us sufficient criteria for judgment, sufficient material for a full participation in the life of large human beings. They bind their projections of men in action to limited conceptions of the possibilities of being human.

Obviously, however, Hemingway has found an adequate stance for expressing the sadness of the basically uncommunicative soul and to give glory to its instants of lonely courage. When he depicts the isolated man, he knows whereof he speaks and the simplistic prose manner which he derives from Gertrude Stein serves him well. (He was a nice boy, a good pupil, she notes maliciously.) He describes a static condition, not an act of becoming. His "moments of truth" are plateaus. The consequence of revelation is a fortified stoic acceptance of mortality. He gives us a partial truth about the human condition.

Why then does so much of his work make us feel like a rainy Sunday afternoon? What depresses us finally is this vision of human possibility—one of violent compartmentalization, strict limits, and no growth possible. On the occasions when he seeks to express a sense of people coming meaningfully together, he falls into an embarrassing purple rhetoric, as in the sleeping-bag scenes of *For Whom the Bell Tolls* or in the biography of the battered old love-hungry soldier in *Across the River and Into the Trees*. This is not to derogate his great achievement, the one which is responsible for his popularity and his enduring projection of an aspect of life in the twentieth century. From beginning to end, he has spun out a continuous moral romance about the lonely man striving for dignity, grace, and compassion within a world populated by real sharks and imaginary tender boys and girls.

The Cataloguers: John O'Hara is a good example. They observe. They make the discovery of the trivial—it is *most* important; in fact, even the important is merely trivial; the trivial tells us all we need know. They soothe us with sociology. They lay us to rest with details of tailoring and brand names. Their predominant cast of mind is a sentimental passivity toward the dead weight of facts, which are seen quantitatively, and the contents of a closet are given the same loyal inventory as the two-headed contents of a bed.

The Outer Essence Boys: Truman Capote and the chattering poets of decoration. A paragraph is a hammock in which words copulate prettily. Society is a meeting of birds on the wing. Put more formally, they do what bad poets do: they use words as if they were things and not signs representing acts and things. They drop the object of narrative prose, which is to make sense about human action, and replace it with a prettifying function. They are interior decorators for sentences. We can't all be William Faulkner, Katherine Anne Porter, or even Carson McCullers, but each and every one of us can aspire to be Speed Lamkin.

The Daintily Involved Observers of Aspects: This is the *New Yorker* fashion, although its best writers, such as John Cheever and Robert Coates, do something more. It is a variety of corporate prose less solemn-chuckly than the *Time-Life* product, but no more able to bear the full weight of experience. The *New Yorker* stylists are marvelously shy about the world. They blush before experience, but have learned graceful ways toward it, with shrewd notings of intonation and the vagaries of expression. Parts stand for wholes, although there seems to be a law of expression—the smaller the part, the larger the whole. Finally summoning up their courage before fleeing, these writers offer a pox on life in the last paragraph.

The Common Style Fellas: Herman Wouk proudly claims to write the "common style." This cottony diction, also worked with varying degrees of efficiency by Sloan Wilson and Cameron Hawley, is the great current success. These people are the just-plain-Bills of literature, producing an upper-middle-class soap opera for the readers of Luce magazines and subscribers to the Book-of-the-Month Club's service. They love what-is, whether it be the Navy, the suburb, or the corporation, and come forward to swear their allegiance without quaver or quibble. There may be some touch of nonsense in the process, for the flesh is weak, but they rinse and bleach it all for us in the end.

It is the latter, the "common style," which enjoys the greatest success today. By the phrase "common style" is meant uninvolved, unambitious, "traditional" English diction, without excesses of feeling or rhetoric, suitable to describing the lives of people who want nothing to change, nothing to stop, just let's all pull together, hup-two-three, on to America's last frontier—Adjustment. Those who write the common style show us how to avoid adventure, giving us just enough of it along the way to keep us titillated. It is a manner of withdrawal. They use the tricks of plot to replace action, the display of hysteria to justify emotions treated by Equanil, the questioning of moral assumptions in order to tell us that these questions can be avoided. The method consists in the ejaculatio praecox of drama: clear out before we feel something! The result here too, of course, is a safe but jaded withdrawal from feeling, which is seen as dangerous. (Passion builds and renews only *after* we have submitted to it utterly.)

The artisans of the common style often, like all good engineers, borrow techniques. Particularly they have mastered the cataloguing skill; occasionally they seem for paragraphs at a time almost as delicate as the *New Yorker* stylists; more rarely they imitate a Hemingway growl or a Capote fruitiness. But they turn these methods to their own ends, and go plodding on through their scenarios for adjustment. Flat-footed sentence dogs flat-footed sentence; limp paragraph folds into limp paragraph; the rhythm of phrase prepares us for the dénouement, which is a calculated marriage, a comfortable job, a saving of the company. Form follows function.

The function is to assure us that the lowest common denominator of personality and experience is all we need. The common-style artisans give us an ideal of comfortable conforming ways. The package is all wrapped up and ready to wear; in fact, as easy as old shoes.

The mysterious longing of individuals to create and renew is excised with an almost surgical brutality and precision—although, funnily enough, the American reader can teach these writers much about that of which the novelist is supposed to have special knowledge. American readers are drinkers and sometimes addicts; Americans love jazz and fast driving and secluded corners; with all the itch to conform, Americans are still trying to burst the bonds of isolation by various sorts of violent experiences, including art.

Why then do so many readers find comfort in the dry apotheosis of Marjorie Morningstar's frigidity? How can Sloan Wilson get away with a billion copies of his pettish smugness in the job, the house, the rich aunt, the old wartime affair "talked out" between husband and wife? The great novelists have always given us, before anything else, before all morality and sociology, a sense of the richness of possibility. Why do so many novelists fear the mystery of personality?

Well, first of all, they always have. Besides, life is hard enough without going out looking for challenges. In an impoverished time, palliated by plenty but worried all the same, there is a generalized loss of the sense for creative activity. Nothing more than anxiety inhibits the power to do, to make, to invent, to admit. When your belly is constricted by worry, oatmeal goes down most comfortably. Novelists are human beings more than they are anything else. The mystery of personality is a mystery: isolation, incomprehension, flashes of lightning, cold and hot, danger,

danger, danger. To enter deeply into a dark place involves the risk of coming out where you won't see things as they were. In novels as in life, we cannot eliminate emotion utterly and remain human; but we can replace deep involvements by passing safely from the stage of titillation to that of being jaded without crossing through commitment. We live this way, we write these books, we read them in order to say: *I'm safe, I really am, and I'm pleased about it!* (We keep on renewing the experience because secretly we are not pleased.) Thus Sloan Wilson can declare that his novel expresses his sense for a world which has treated him "pretty well" —wars, bombs, a third of a nation watching Ed Sullivan, all of it. Better forget about adventuring, he means to say; better accept a stereotyped image of desire; better be attentive to the media and take the profit in subsidiary rights.

The novel at its best is a large perspective on life in society— large because the hero's doings are important and because the novelist is deeply concerned with the careers of his people. *Ulysses,* for example, has difficulties of manner, but is not in its conception hermetic. Leopold Bloom is a representative, poignant, and troubling instance of city-dwelling man; his fretting and wanderings in Dublin bring to us the challenge and limitations of our own intelligence, ambition, and ability to love. James Joyce's personal voice here is many-focused, as true personality always is, not the pale self-contemplation, blank and onanistic, which the seventeen-year-old thinks of as the pursuit of himself; nor is it the cruelly partial view of the writer fleeing his largest intelligence. It is a lyric reverie *in the light of* the wide world of society.

What is that grit out of a unique individual which somehow provokes the novel of largest general significance? The nature of the writer's involvement with his material (which consists of all that he knows of life) suggests another clue. For complex psychological reasons, many novelists have been unavowed Platonists, philosophical idealists, possessed of a spectator theory of reality. That is, life has meaning as the shadows on Plato's cave have meaning—as flickering glimpses through fire of something beyond life, something perfect and unchanging and finally unknowable by men. Their world is a system deduced from unknown premises. *Unknown*—this paradox torments them. How can deductions be made without defined terms? Therefore they look for moral abstractions, categories, faiths, anything that can place them outside the tormenting flux of time and sensuality. Perhaps they become doctrinaire religionists or Marxists. They take their stand as viewers, as unwinders. What is the effect on their novels? Well, some of these writers are great ones, like Proust and Henry James, engaged in enterprises of passive integration in order to give some "symbolic" sense to the unruly factness of life. They shrink; still they cannot avoid rendering this dense, combative, time-ridden teeming. Despite their static position, Proust and James at their best project a moving image of desire.

But in anything less than a master, the type of self-absorption in moody fantasies is crippling. We may be hypnotized by it; we all have deep impulses to passivity before the fright of time; but an aspiration to perfection expressed as static clutching finally leads to paralysis. We stiffen; we are isolated. Platonism here parallels what the psychoanalysts call "fixation"—a retreat to impossibly perfect and unchanging gratifications or frustrations. We sneeze, we wheeze, our bodies protest.

Let us now set the empirical novelist against the deductive one. "Love" is not an abstraction to be encompassed by definition; it is this Jack and Jane, that Bud and Joy—look and see! The novelist is not studying shadows for some ultimate reality beyond earth; he accepts that the shadows themselves give him all that he can know; in fact, that they are enough; in fact, they are not shadows—they are thick reality itself and a marvel to behold.

There is the lesson of a Welsh phrase: "The rent that's due to love"—you must pay and pay and pay, relentlessly giving yourself and making others give, too. The category "Love" does not exist; it can be merely rented, never owned; it is unpossessable in any final way. Like the medieval cathedral, like a child, like love, the great novel gives a sense of not yet completed life within whatever its perfections of design. Attempting to offer the sense of life, a novel is always in process. You can't step in the same story twice. When the writer sits down to his desk in the morning, there is nothing so safe and deadly as knowing exactly what comes next. If he is a real novelist by temper of imagination, but weakly hopes to have the security of a controlled symmetry, he will find that his characters shake their fists into the crooks of their elbows, set his schemes on their tails, ruthlessly rewrite him. All that he is makes his people all that they are, but they are endowed with the kind of independence which defiant children have when they leave a good home. Fortified by their parents to make their own way, they are most loyal in being most free.

The mystery of personality can be defined again and again, and then redefined: that's what mysteries are for. A jittery scientist has defined personality as "the index of inefficiency." Machines are both efficient and free of caprice, he assures himself; therefore personality is a negative quantity with respect to intention, plan, goals; therefore the ideal of Science must be the elimination of personality in favor of socially governed ends. How are the ends to be determined? By what criteria are they judged? By the efficient, impersonal needs of the smoothly running society. Needs? *Needs?* Why, for Plato's sake, pal, that's more circular (in logical terms) and hysterical (in psychological lingo) than any aesthetic rant.

The Mystery of Personality in the Novel

Personality is prickly against definition. Let us return to the novel. In novels the mystery will make itself manifest as an individual, unsocialized perception, compassion, hatred, and love— a congeries of unique relationships with unique creatures and events. Despite the difficulties of definition, we know that the lonely, self-devouring ego is not personality and neither is the busy radar-flaunting opportunist: they are both flights from that mystery. They are willed, not willing; worked on, not working. They are not mysterious, either: they are explainable products. They can be comic and pathetic, even typical of a society—never heroic, tragic, or representative of aspiration (which is also a part of the twentieth century archetype).

However, the man moving in consciousness and contemplation of his will—really conscious and watching, really moving and committed—is the personality capable of mysteries. He signifies. His passion defines freedom for all of us. His is the will which, in type, reaches to the divine maximum, where God made something from nothing, the heavens and earth popping out of his pride in six days, not seven—on the seventh day he gloated; at a slightly less monstrous level, Balzac created the *Le Père Goriot* in fifty-eight days, complete with Vautrin swarming over Rastignac's soul. Love, ambition, power under the sun of mortality! These are the issues; the great heroes of fiction meet these risks head on—as we all do, but too often also face down.

The novelist must reach for the grownup, risking, athletic personality, surely must in some way be this person, in order to find a hero who gives the sense of men at their best on earth: and catch him finally where his great gifts do not suffice: this is tragedy. American life is rich in suggestions of tragic themes: the man in politics is cracked by his ambition—but really involved, not floating above politics; the man in business fails against the fierce appetite of the devouring business world—but really struggling and pretty fierce himself, while not mistaking the business world for the whole of life; the lover is lost by love, as it is perhaps still possible to be, but by a love which is health and desire for a woman worth desiring and defeated by the natural strangeness of human beings. And it would not be stretching the essential definition of tragedy to show the possibilities of individual triumph in all these struggles.

Personality is a key, not a twitch.

Without personality, manifested by what is called style, there is no significant touching.

Personality in the novel leads to communion with others, a meaningful individual participation in the common career. Otherwise, despite all brilliance, emotion is reduced to the self-loathing of a Céline or the self-aggrandizement of the crippled perspectives mentioned earlier. The individual is more than the common style's stock-figure cartoon of Everyman in gray flannel. And of course the individual is more than the cracked-up romantic poet at three o'clock in the morning in the dark night of his soul.

We should expect the fragmentation of self in the modern novel, just as we expect it in the man bound to a factory or office, within a social structure which cannot use the largest capacities of millions of individuals. Writers are responsive people: the complexities of the experience of being an American in 1957 are enough to tempt all of us to turn to partial, limited, maybe soothing half-views. What a dangerous thing to be all present and awake before the front page of the daily newspaper!

Can some novelists stand up against their confusion and fright?

Yes, and even with courage, humor, and a will to do good work. Without naming specific writers, I suggest that the contemporary American novel is still the best place to look for instances of lives which seek to be whole and unafraid.

Confidence and freedom of style are good signs of a writer's taking a chance. A style which attempts to use all a writer knows to tell all he can imagine involves a moral stance in favor of intelligence and liberty and risk taking. With their varying defects and capacities, such writers have this in common: they are individuals, not products; they are making a way, not accepting a road; they do not flinch before the mystery of personality, or when they do, they give signs of knowing that there is something vital left out. Their failures are peculiarly ungracious: they intend otherwise. They will try again next time.

At its best, the art of the novel tells us more than we can find out elsewhere about love and death. We commune together before a guiding image of the always unfulfilled possibilities of life on earth. We are therefore in continual need of the dangerous, destructive moralist which the great novelist is.

Mark Harris
Easy Does It Not

After you have made a diagnosis of the mechanical faults that may be causing you to read slowly, you are ready to apply remedial measures. . . . For all practice you should be sure to use EXTREMELY EASY AND RELATIVELY WORTHLESS READING MATERIAL, usually stories.
—*Reading Rapidly and Well*, Wrenn and Cole

LET ME BEGIN in close.

I happen to own a left-handed baseball pitcher named Henry Wiggen. His teammates on the New York Mammoths call him "Author." I own the Mammoths, too. Indeed, I own the whole damn league, all the cities and all the players and all their wives and children. It is great fun. In collaboration, Henry and I have written three novels about our league.

Henry's left arm is his fortune, but his ear is his soul. He listens not to what people say but to what they mean. His report upon what he hears is frank, but he is armed against reprisal: his enemies, since they are invariably malicious (which is to say, stupid), have not the ears to know they have been condemned. If the reader is himself without ears (which is to say, untrained to read) he will think Henry untrained to write. He will think Henry is nothing but a baseball player.

Among Henry's admirers are several gentlemen with the rank of Associate Editor or better at *Life* magazine. One day, on behalf of these gentlemen, a letter was sent to me asking whether, by chance, I had available a Henry Wiggen story which I might send to them for possible publication in the issue for July 2, 1956. I replied No, I had none at the moment. But I had an *idea*, I said. I outlined my idea, and they were delighted. They formalized matters with my agent, and *she* was delighted. Soon afterward I received an advance payment of $1,000. (Total payment for the story, upon acceptance, was to be at the rate of fifty cents a word, a sum likely to approach $10,000, or almost twice my annual salary as Instructor in English at San Francisco State College.) This $1,000 was mine to keep regardless of whether *Life* published the story: I was required only to deliver a manuscript.

I did not spend it. I put it in a safe place. Had I spent it I would have been committed to the completion of a project which, in the course of writing, I may have discovered was best left uncompleted. I thus reserved for myself the right of abandonment, for if my story should fail I could return to *Life* its $1,000 and keep to myself the unsuccessful manuscript.

The invitation could not have come at a more propitious time. We were in the midst of a busy semester at school, while about the house an extraordinary social season was in progress. These are, for me, the proper conditions for work, when morning and evening are crowded with talk and press, when I can make of my day a sandwich of four silent afternoon hours. For some weeks I lived a triangle, traveling from home to school, from school to a rented apartment where I worked on the *Life* story, thence home again.

The rented apartment was situated on the third floor of a dwelling on San Francisco's Downey Street. Below, children played in the St. Agnes schoolyard. Their cry was with me, and it was appropriate to my purpose, for I was writing a story whose climax occurs at a baseball game, July 4, 1956, in Moors Stadium (I own it) in New York City, in the presence of the cry of many people. The cry from below was a persistent guide toward the finale I was pursuing. It prevented me from straying.

Yet when I wandered to the window, as from time to time I did, I saw how this was no crowd at all, how it was, rather, children one by one, separate and special, even as my own children are, to me at least, separate and special. I write, I think, of persons, not of crowds. Thus, as I wrote, my ear knew the voice of my subject, and my eye knew its image.

I saw from the window a society whole and complete, insistent upon its laws and traditions, yet not unwilling, now and then, to experiment, a society of followers and leaders, and, occasionally, of rebels and heretics, a body of men and women between the ages of six and twelve possessing within it the genius both to conserve and to progress, to govern, regulate, restrict, limit, resist, yet also to improvise and advance. You will find many such playgrounds in the City of San Francisco, here at the Western edge of the Western World. "This habit," De Tocqueville found, "may be traced even in the schools, where the children in their games are wont to submit to rules which they have themselves established, and to punish misdemeanors which they have themselves defined."

Please do not mistake me. I do not believe we have achieved, in the United States of America, a community of perfect order. I do not share *Life*'s confidence that we are "the most successful society in human history." But although in politics I usually oppose the incumbency, recoil from prevailing tastes, and find myself unable to affiliate in spirit or even in fact with any power bloc larger than the company of a few friends, my sense of comfort—of belonging to the nation—is more than illusion. I do not think I am of those writers who, *Life* says, "feel surrounded by sinister, hostile forces, even a Philistine conspiracy to control their thoughts. . . ." My books have regularly been published by capitalists and read by Philistines, and one of them has even been beamed to the nation on television at considerable expense by the United States Steel Corporation.

Everything, it seemed, was right, my days arranged, money in escrow. At last, after fifteen years at hard labor, I was to become national! In July my characters, my vision, I myself, would become known to 5,714,000 readers. I who had always felt myself to be living not quite without, and yet not quite within, the mainstream of the national life, was at last acceptable.

My plot was this:

A young lady writes to Henry Wiggen from "somewhere out West" to tell him that she will be in New York to watch the Mammoths play on July 4th. Henry is her hero. But Henry has a wife, and for this reason (he says) he attempts to transfer the young lady's affection from himself to Thurston Woods, inevitably called "Piney," a twenty-year-old catcher with a passion for women of the Hollywood type, fast motorcycles, and low-slung automobiles.

We follow the young lady's cross-country journey, wherein she is endangered but never quite violated (she says). She is delayed for a time at The Geographical Center of the United States Motel, whose owner's intentions toward her are ambiguous but who finally delivers her safely to New York. He has sworn upon a stack of Bibles that he will do so, and so (of course) he does.

Piney Woods discovers, when the girl arrives, that she is no beauty. His dream has overshot reality. He begins to discover, however, that love and charm may reside even within a form less divine than Hollywood specifies. He learns, too, that mechanical progress may ring hollow.

I wrote my story in four-hour stints, cooled it, retyped it, and mailed it to Ralph Graves, the Associate Editor with whom I was working. I was less than wholly satisfied, and as I awaited Mr. Graves's reaction my doubt mounted. It became apparent to me that, as I had written the story, I had been fearful of the manner in which I was dealing with certain subjects. Should I, perhaps, have avoided motorcycles and Bibles? Is not a man on a motorcycle, reading a Bible, the very image of the ideal citizen in the most successful society in human history? My fears had cramped my style. Would not a little prudence have been wise? Think how many imprudent things I might afterward do and say with $10,000 in my pocket!

Mr. Graves was delighted with the story. But he was returning it for revision. He sent a six-page letter with recommendations so technically admirable as to be irresistible. He sent, also, another $1,000. I have worked with fine editors over the years, and I have come to depend upon them—with Walter Pistole at Reynal & Hitchcock, with Louis Simpson, John Maloney, and Hiram Haydn at Bobbs-Merrill, with Al Hart at Macmillan, and with Joe Fox and Harold Strauss at Knopf. To this class, I now saw, Ralph Graves belongs, and to him my story is dedicated: that which had been a good-enough story was fashioned, because he scolded, into something much more. Forget wordage, he said; do a novel if you can't do a story. Rest your fears, uncramp, shake loose, let fly, go fuller, go deeper, and this I did, and my story was soon a story no more but a novel (at the very least a $15,000 novel, computed at *Life* rates). Its plot was the plot I have described, Bibles and motorcycles and all, but it now had space to move and turn and wheel and sound and echo in. I felt it leaping and racing, joyous in its release from confinement, and

I worked, now, not four hours a day but fourteen, long after the schoolyard was dark and the children home asleep, and when it was done I knew that I had done something I shall never quite do again, and my friends at *Life* knew what I had done, and they sent it up—up to the man upstairs—and he said No.

In a twinkling was a small fortune lost. Had I ever really counted upon it in the first place, and begun to live the life of a man worth fifty cents a word, I would have been in serious difficulty with myself and with my art. Fortunately, the $13,000 I did not have was essential neither to the pride nor to the happiness of my family, and we largely shared the sentiment of our friend the novelist Donald Wetzel, who wrote to me: "Anyhow I know you got paid something for it. I think, well good, just like when I tried to get a job there and didn't, bad as I needed one. I mean I still thought, well good."

I composed a dedication page, inserted it in the manuscript, and asked my agent to deliver the whole to my publisher, Alfred A. Knopf, Inc. Harold Strauss, my editor at Knopf, found it, he wrote (my immodesty appals me, but this is relevant, I think), "a minor American masterpiece. Not to publish it . . . would be a disservice to American literature." He then sent it to *his* man upstairs—to Mr. Knopf—from whom I soon received a most flattering note: "I have read *A Ticket for a Seamstitch* with delight. It is a true work of art and I think absolutely flawless within the limits you have set for yourself."

Life published, in its issue for July 2, 1956, instead of my story, an excerpt ("one of the best episodes") from a novel by William Brinkley, an Assistant Editor on its staff. "Good-humored and broadly satirical," the novel was shortly to be distributed by the Book-of-the-Month Club, a factor which I assume left a strong impression upon the man upstairs, for the excerpt was preceded by a detailed account of the book's adventure in high finance:

M-G-M had bought it for $400,000 ("a sliding scale on movie profits"), Denmark, England, and Holland had bought it; it "promises to be financially one of the most successful books of 1956. . . . Brinkley is expected to make a total of $600,000." The novel subsequently ascended, in four weeks, to the top of the *New York Times* best-seller list, where it spent the summer.

I saw, everywhere, its advertisement: "It's got the whole country laughing!"

I read what I could, and I barely smiled, and as I sought among my friends confirmation of my own judgment I came to realize that they had not read it and did not plan to, that "the whole country" was somebody somewhere else. A few of my friends had turned its pages in bookstores, as one will, had read *in* it, not laughed, closed it, and forgotten it. Yet we are not remote from life. We laugh, we have our passions.

In time, Mr. Brinkley disappeared, and the advertisements ceased. "I want to do fiction," says Mr. Brinkley, "learn how to write fiction." It is an engaging modesty, all the more affecting because his faith is the faith of innocence: if, at thirty-eight, Mr. Brinkley can really write no better than he writes now, he will never learn. He is certain that writing is easy, that there is nothing to it, that you put words together and form a vague picture of an action, and there you have it—lo!—writing. He did it easily, and it was easily read. When, in the autumn, I returned to school I discovered that my entering freshmen had read Mr. Brinkley, and that they had liked him. "Easy reading," they said.

My experience became meaningful to me, now, in a way it had not been. The passage of my manuscript through the uppermost offices of *Life* provided me with authority for this account. Who could have asked more for $13,000? I see at last a chief difficulty of American fiction: I see that a magazine like *Life* objects less to controversial subject matter than to difficult style. *Not irreverence, but craftsmanship, dismays the editors of mass media.*

There is easy reading. And there is literature. There are easy writers, and there are writers. There are people whose ears have never grown, or have fallen off, or have merely lost the power to listen. And there are people with ears.

II

I see, in GROSSINGER NEWS-NOTES, which I studiously read every Sunday on the Resorts page of the *New York Times*, the following: "Long distance honors of the week go to . . . Leon Carat and his sister, Lena, who are here from Paris, France." And only this moment my eye catches, in the same advertisement, word to the effect that "Herman WOUK, brilliant author," was at Grossinger's during the week Leon and Lena were there.

Or I call to mind that triumphant joke about the hopeful *Reader's Digest* contributor—he who had sexual intercourse with a bear in an iron lung for the FBI and found God.

Do you laugh? I laugh. My friends laugh. If you have ears you have a sense of the world, you know where Paris is, you have never gone to Grossinger's, you are not astonished to learn that Mr. Wouk vacations there, you do not read the *Digest*. I once heard Groucho Marx, on the radio, attempt to convey the *Digest* joke. His studio audience responded with a profound silence. (Probably you have never been a member of a studio audience.) Yet the joke has traveled round and round and round the country, and raised, I am sure, a million voices in laughter. It delights men and women whose ears have caught the rhythm of the *Digest*, but who do not subscribe.

The life of our literature depends, like the life of a superb joke, upon private transmission, not upon television, radio, or magazines. The novelist depends upon that relatively small audience which brings to reading a frame of reference, a sophistication, a level of understanding not lower than the novelist's own. He cannot hope to touch the reader who comes in innocence, who must be told upon each occasion where Paris is, who demands, in short, that the novelist be easy, that he not require the reader to exert any part of himself but his eyeballs.

Such a reader is hopeless. "You must depend upon the reader to stretch his mind," Elizabeth Janeway once warned me. "You cannot stretch it for him." This I believe, and I resist, as *true* novelists do, the injunction (usually a worried editor's) to be clearer, to be easier, to explain, if I feel that the request is for the convenience of the reader at the expense of craft. The novelist jealous of his craft cannot write the Brinkley line:

" 'Gentlemen,' he said humorously, switching on his electric-light smile . . ."

Rather, he writes for the reader who will decide for himself whether the speaker speaks with humor, and what kind of smile the speaker smiles. Or, if the novelist describes a smile, he will choose to do so with precision. He cannot reduce himself, cannot believe he is saying anything when he tells you, as Mr. Brinkley does, that someone sits "silent . . . as an owl," that someone "had the aspect of a man who tangled with one of the Seabee's bull-dozers," or that people "looked like the survivors of a fierce naval engagement." This is to say nothing, nothing at all, to hurry words onto paper as if they do not matter.

The novelist will set you down among his people, and he will leave you to inhabit their world with them, and you will perceive for yourself the habits and assumptions which shape motives. Shakespeare supplies no stage directions beyond bare information to the effect that people enter and exit, assigning to our imagination the task of forming from the speech of his people our notions of their character.

Robert Coughlan, a Staff Writer for *Life*, complains in *The*

Private World of William Faulkner, that in *A Fable* "nothing is
revealed directly if it can be done by reflection; episodes and
conversations begin without prior references to known events or
thoughts; nothing is said clearly if it can be obfuscated; characters appear from nowhere and disappear to nowhere; moti-
vation and character development are inexplicable. The book,
on the whole, seems demented." Even so, Mr. Coughlan "somehow" was "deeply and personally if irrationally involved in a
great and infinitely tragic event."

What is wanted? That something infinitely tragic has been
achieved is commendable, apparently, but the book is demented
because Mr. Faulkner did not produce infinite tragedy straight-
forwardly, chronologically, systematically—did not make of his
work "easy reading."

The charge against Mr. Faulkner is that he is difficult, and
that he is afflicted by a "cosmic pessimism," a phrase which Mr.
Coughlan asserts has no meaning. Yet it has meaning, and you
have encountered it if you have been reading better books than
Easy Reading Made Simpler Than Ever; and the greater a novelist's awareness of language, of time, and of place, the greater will
be his need for a form and a style to capture his mood.

"The habit of expression," Henry Adams observed, "leads to
the search for something to express." Habit and search lead to
complexity. Complexity, in turn, may shrink one's audience, at
least over the short run, but time and labor teach us that Mr.
Faulkner's world is not a "private world" at all, but one to which
anyone may admit himself if he looks upon reading less as a
passive act than as a pursuit requiring the effort of concentration.

The novelist in search of his own best self continues in his
conviction. He persuades himself that his defiance of the temptation to increase personal comfort at the sacrifice of craft assures
him the distant reward of fame. It is his faith, his religion. He
remembers an early day when he was called "promising," and

he knows that although he has been moving beyond "promise" his audience has failed to widen. Yet perhaps it has solidified, and he may live to hear, as Faulkner has, the praise of a generation which has discovered that his seeming difficulty is in fact the inevitable result of his ambition to express a difficult idea.

You may not admire Faulkner. You may prefer Hemingway, James, Katherine Anne Porter, or someone else whose ears have grown fantastic big. Whoever it is, if he or she is truly good he is good not alone upon the basis of two or three enduring works but because of his service to a literary principle whose foremost article of faith declares, "I write. Let the reader learn to read." And our best writers are indebted to those readers who by strenuous labor learn to see how those prior references, which Mr. Coughlan cannot locate, are not only present but are embedded in exactly the place—and in the only place—Mr. Faulkner could possibly have put them.

Whether the contentment with easy reading is more pernicious in our own age than it was in any other I do not know. I cannot really think so. People with neither the will nor the means to grow ears have never sustained literature. It is disturbing, however, to discover presumably literate people, some of whom wear the uniform of teachers of literature, who parade secure in the belief that they can read books without *reading* them. They read reviews. They watch television. They will feel confident that they have read *A Farewell to Arms* after they have seen the motion picture produced by Mr. David O. Selznick: he read "résumés of appraisals by book critics."

They say, I cannot understand your book. I think you left something out.

But everything is there. Everything you need to know is there.

I am told, It has baseball players in it.

Yes.

Then it is about baseball.

No.

They say, I see where your book was on television. *Now* you are going places.

But I left nothing out. It is simply that I cannot explain. A novel is drama, not report; scene, not exposition. You will pardon me if, in my obsession with craftsmanship, I cause my people to speak to each other, not to the reader. "Good morning, Mr. Smith, chief engineer here at Atlas Tool Works." When I hear such a speech I will write it down.

I am a storyteller, not a sociologist or linguist or psychologist. I do not educate nor reform. When I am writing my novels I leave my morality in the other room, and I therefore plead with you to differentiate between the characters of a book and the character of its author. Until you appreciate viewpoint you cannot read.

I cannot tell you when to laugh. If you say, "I did not laugh," I can only reply, "Grow ears."

I shall not *tell* you anything. I shall allow you to eavesdrop on my people, and sometimes they will tell the truth and sometimes they will lie, and you must determine for yourself when they are doing which. You do this every day. Your butcher says, "This is the best," and you reply, "That's *you* saying it." Shall my people be less the captive of their desires than your butcher? I can *show* much, but show only, and if you have ears you will do what Mr. Shakespeare and Mr. Hemingway have taught us to do: you will vivify dialogue by setting your own music to the words, bringing to your own reading your own creative intelligence, your own imagination. You will no more expect the novelist to tell you precisely *how* something is said than you will expect him to stand by your chair and hold your book.*

I know of no serious novelist now at work who is deliberately

* In a half-page of Brinkley: "Ensign Siegel said blankly," "Ensign Siegel said absently," "the exec exclaimed," "the exec whipped out," "the exec shouted" ("with a canny smile"), "the exec said ferociously," "Siegel said urgently," then "fervently," etc.—*Life*, July 2, 1956, p. 124.

mysterious or obscure. If, for example, he distorts time, he does so because his events, he feels, thereby gain force in the telling. The reader who reads will sooner or later see that the novelist has done what he has done for the sake of his story. In conversation we do the same, compressing, rearranging, careless of sequence in the interest of the sharper truth we fashion by dramatizing experience. The novelist's rebellion is not against clock nor calendar but against the form and manner of the novels he has read, and against, most of all, his own last novel. The serious novelist chiefly resists the mixture as before, his own mixture or anybody else's, desiring for his newest work exactly that precious quality heralded weekly but delivered much less often: originality.

Nor will he tell you what his novel *means*. All the actions of life have their themes, their morals, that "natural symbolism of reality" of which Mary McCarthy speaks. A novelist's proper role is only to show an action, or a series of related actions. For people with ears each day, each encounter, each contest of person with person, informs life, and the novelist but extends experience, carrying his reader to new places and to new acquaintance. The symbols await analysis and explication, but this is the work of the reader, not of the writer. You cannot say, "It gripped me, it moved me, I couldn't put it down. What does it mean?" For then you are saying that the writer did his job, but that you have not done yours.

"I write. Let the reader learn to read." I must be as skillful as I can. I am obliged to be the best craftsman I can be. I must be free to choose my subject and my language, and I am at liberty to experiment, to grow, to express, if need be, the complexity of my experience with whatever resources are at hand. I will talk baby talk to babies and dog talk to dogs, but I cannot tell you in baby talk or dog talk of the excitement of being an adult human being in a world so wondrous with hope and sorrow and loyalty and defeat and anguish and delight.

All of us who *write* once made the decision to write out the best that is in us. It has nothing to do with Integrity, only with taste and preference. Loath to tape our ears to our skulls, we said, instead, We shall let our ears grow up and away and see what happens.

We want to tell the jokes we want to tell, and we can tell them only to people with ears to listen, people who will bring to the evening talents to challenge our own, who will work as goddam hard to read as we work who write.

Wright Morris
The Territory Ahead

Suggestions as to where it lies:

> Let me live where I will, on this side is the city, on that the wilderness, and ever I am leaving the city more and more and withdrawing into the wilderness. I should not lay so much stress on this fact if I did not believe that something like this is the prevailing tendency of my countrymen. —THOREAU

> But I reckon I got to light out for the Territory ahead of the rest, because Aunt Sally she's going to adopt and civilize me, and I can't stand it. I been there before. —HUCK FINN

> One realm we have never conquered: the pure present. One great mystery of time is terra incognita to us: the instant. The most superb mystery we have hardly recognized: the immediate, instant self. The quick of all time is the instant. The quick of all the universe, of all creation, is the incarnate, carnal self. Poetry gave us the clue: free verse: Whitman. Now we know.
>
> —D. H. LAWRENCE

I want to know if I can live with what I know and only with
that.   —ALBERT CAMUS

TECHNIQUE AND RAW MATERIAL

"God alive, Sir Knight of the Mournful Countenance," said
Sancho, "I cannot bear in patience some of the things that your
Grace says! Listening to you, I come to think that all you have
told me about deeds of chivalry and winning kingdoms and be-
stowing islands and other favors and dignities is but wind and lies,
all buggery or humbuggery or whatever you choose to call it. For
when anyone hears your Grace saying that a barber's basin is
Mambrino's helmet, and after four days you still insist that it is,
what is he to think except that such a one is out of his mind? I have
the basin in my bag, all crushed and dented. I'm taking it home to
have it mended so that I can trim my beard into it, if God is only
good enough to let me see my wife and children again some day."

We have that barber's basin, more crushed and dented than
ever, among us today. It symbolizes the state of the imagination
in the raw material world of facts. Like Sancho, the modern
temper distrusts the processes of the imagination, but it has great
faith in the alchemy of the laboratory. High octane and low
imagination are the order of the day.

The romantic agony of the poet has been displaced by the
agony of the test tube—the compulsive commitments of the
poet have given way to the compulsive behavior of atomic fission.
The hallmark of the true agony is that extinction is preferable
to self-examination. The end of life, that is, public and private,
is preferable to the end of the pursuit of such knowledge.

Technique and raw material are essential to both the study and
the laboratory. By raw material I mean that comparatively crude
ore that has not been processed by the imagination—what we
refer to as *life*, or as experience, in contrast to art. By technique
I mean the way that the artist smelts this material down for human
consumption.

A new world, in these terms, will contain more raw material than an old one. America, that is, is rawer than Europe. This rawness is comparative, however, since the brave new world that the explorer discovers contains, on the whole, only what he comes prepared to find. But a permissible illusion of rawness exists on each frontier. And in a nation of expanding frontiers, the illusion of rawness expands along with them. Technique, in this pioneer picture, is therefore little more than a clearing operation—the raw material is the thing, and the technique is a method of collecting it. There usually appears to be an inexhaustible supply of it. But if you happen to run out of it where you are, why then you move on to where it is waiting. It *exists*, that is. It is not something the artist conjures up.

If the world is a collection of crude barbers' basins which the artist must transmute into gold, Cervantes gives us a lesson in how this trick is done. At a moment of crisis in the imagination itself—at one pole Cervantes, at the other Shakespeare—we are taken behind the scenes and shown how the imagination works. We are not merely told that the world is a stage, but how it operates. Technique and raw material are dramatized at the moment that the shaping imagination is aware of itself. We see the way in which the world—in Whitehead's sense—is processed into reality. The transitory, illusive facts are shaped into a fiction of permanence. At the moment that the mind takes the step we think of as characteristically modern, we are taken offstage, into the very wings of the mind itself. We are allowed to see the world, as the raw material, and Don Quixote, the transforming technician. The author, whom we do not see, is the discipline that turns the Mournful Knight's mad antics to the service of the heart's desire, the intelligence. Both technique and raw material—the processed fiction and the raw fact—confront each other in Don Quixote and Sancho, a legend of the labyrinthine ways of the imagination itself.

II

The history of fiction, its pursuit of that chimera we describe as reality, is a series of imaginative triumphs made possible through technique. In *Mimesis,* Erich Auerbach has charted this course from Homer to Joyce. In esthetic terms, *facts* are those sensations that have been convincingly processed by the imagination. They are the materials, the artifacts, so to speak, that we actually possess.

At the summit of technique we have such a craftsman as Joyce. There is so little craft in fiction on this scale that so much craft seems forbidding. Is the end result—we are inclined to ask ourselves—still alive? Is life, real or imaginary, meant to be processed as much as that? In Joyce the dominance of technique over raw material reflects one crisis of the modern imagination. Raw material has literally dissolved into technique.

In *Finnegans Wake* the world of Dublin happens to be the raw material that Joyce puts through his process—but the process, not Dublin, is the thing. It is the process that will give the raw material its enduring form. A parallel transformation is still taking place in what we call modern art. In Manet's portrait of Clemenceau the subject has vanished into the method—the method has become painting itself. Both Dublin and Clemenceau are processed into means, rather than ends, since the artist's problem is not to reconstruct the old, but to construct the new. It is characteristic of the mind of Joyce that the city of Dublin, shaped by his ironic craft, should not merely disappear but prove hard to find.

The brave new world has had its share of able craftsmen, but with the exception of Hawthorne and James, both closely linked to the old, they usually lacked what we would call the master touch. Raw material, usually the rawer the better, seemed to be their forte. On certain rare and unpredictable occasions craft might break through this devotion to raw material, but the resulting masterpiece had about it the air of an accident. Not so much a crafty man-made thing, as a gift from above. The author usually took pains not to repeat it, or to learn from his experience. *Walden, Leaves of Grass, Moby Dick,* and *The Adventures of Huckleberry Finn,* have in common this sense of isolation. Happy or unhappy accidents, something of a mystery to both the author and the public. They resemble some aspect of a natural force—a pond, a river, a demonic whale—rather than something cleverly contrived by man. They seem to have more in common with Niagara Falls, Mammoth Cave, or Old Faithful than with a particular author, or anything so artificial as art. They are wonders, but *natural* wonders, like the Great Stone Face.

This notion of the natural, the unschooled genius who leaps, like a trout, from some mountain stream, seems to be central to our national egotism. It reappears every day in the child—or the backward, untutored adult—who draws, writes, strums a saw or plays a piano without *ever* having taken a lesson. That lessons might corrupt his talent, and ruin his promise, goes without saying. We believe in doing only what comes naturally. Naturally to us.

But those natural moments in which we take so much pride—*Walden, Leaves of Grass, Moby Dick* and *Huck Finn*—are, without exception, moments of grace under pressure, triumphs of craft. The men who produced them are artists, innovators, of the first magnitude. Each of these statements is a contemporary statement, and each is unique. They represent new levels where, in the words of D. H. Lawrence, the work of art can ". . . inform and lead into new places the flow of our sympathetic consciousness, and it can lead our sympathy away in recoil from things gone dead."

If we now ask ourselves under what pressure these moments of grace are achieved, I believe it is the pressure of the raw material itself. Each of these men felt the need to domesticate a continent. In his essay on Hawthorne, Melville observed: "It is not so much paucity as superabundance of material that seems to incapacitate modern authors."

He had reason to know. It was not lack of material that silenced Herman Melville. The metaphysical woods that he found mirrored in the sea, and which drew him to it, of all aspects of the brave new world were the least inhabited.

III

With the passing of the last natural frontier—that series of horizons dissolving westward—the raw-material myth, based, as it is, on the myth of inexhaustible resources, no longer supplies the artisan with lumps of raw life. All of it has been handled. He now inhabits a world of raw-material clichés. His homemade provincial wares no longer startle and amaze the world. As a writer he must meet, and beat, the Old World Masters at their own game. In his "Monologue to the Maestro," Hemingway states the problem in his characteristic manner:

There is no use writing anything that has been written better before unless you can beat it. What a writer in our time has to do is write what hasn't been written before or beat dead men at what they have done. The only way he can tell how he is going is to compete with dead men . . . the only people for a serious writer to compete with are the dead that he knows are good. . . .

With this credo the Portrait of the Artist as a Young American is permanently revised. The provincial is out. The dyed-in-the-wool professional is in. Not only do we have to meet the champ: we have to beat him. That calls, among other things, for knowing who he is. Such a statement could only come from a writer who knows you have to beat the Masters with style and technique, and it is on these terms that he has won his place in the pantheon.

If raw material is so bad, if it is the pitfall and handicap to the artist that I am suggesting, why is it that American writers, through rather than in spite of this handicap, are one of the germinal forces wherever books are read. Here, I think, we have an instructive paradox. It involves us in the problem of good and bad taste. Not the good or bad taste of the artist, but the good or bad taste we find in his raw material. Good taste—*good* in the sense that it is fashionable and decorative—usually indicates an absence of the stuff of life that the artist finds most congenial. Both the Parthenon and the urban apartment decorated with Mondrian and Van Gogh resist more than a passing reference, usually ironic in tone. The over-processed material, what we sense as over-refinement, is an almost fatal handicap to the artist: we feel this handicap in James—not in his mind, but in his material—and it is at a final extremity in Proust. Only a formidable genius, only a formidable technique, can find in such material fresh and vital elements.

Bad taste, on the other hand, is invariably an ornament of vitality, and it is the badness that cries out with meaning, and calls for processing. Raw material and bad taste—the feeling we have that bad taste indicates *raw* material—is part of our persuasion that bad grammar, in both life and literature, reflects *real* life. But bad taste of this sort is hard to find. Bad "good taste" is the world in which we now live.

In reference to Joyce, Harry Levin has said: "The best writing of our contemporaries is not an act of creation, but an act of evocation peculiarly saturated with reminiscences."

This observation pertains to Joyce and Proust as it does to Fitzgerald and his dream of Gatsby, or to Hemingway's Nick on "The Big Two-Hearted River." In our time, that is, nostalgia is not peculiarly American.

But the uses to which the past is put allow us to distinguish between the minor and the major craftsman. The minor artist is usually content to indulge in it. But the labyrinthine reminiscence of Proust is conceptual, *consciously* conceptual, in contrast to the highly unconscious reminiscence in *Huckleberry Finn*. Not *knowing* what he was doing, Mark Twain was under no compulsion to do it again.

Twain's preference for *real* life—*Life on the Mississippi*—is the preference Thoreau felt for facts, the facts of Nature, and Whitman's preference for the man-made artifact. Something *real*. Something the hand, as well as the mind, could grasp. Carried to its conclusion this preference begins and ends right where we find it—in autobiography. On this plane raw material and art appear to be identical. *I was there, I saw, and I suffered*, said Whitman, sounding the note, and the preference is still dear to the readers of the *Saturday Evening Post*. Wanting no nonsense, only facts, we make a curious discovery. Facts are like faces. There are millions of them. They are disturbingly alike. It is the imagination that looks behind the face, as well as looks out of it.

Letting the evidence speak for itself, the facts, that is, of the raw-material myth, the indications are that it destroys more than it creates. It has become a dream of abuse rather than use. We are no longer a raw-material reservoir, the marvel and despair of less fortunate cultures, since our only inexhaustible resource at the moment is the cliché. An endless flow of clichés, tirelessly processed for mass-media consumption, now give a sheen of vitality to what is either stillborn or secondhand. The hallmark of these clichés is a processed sentimentality. The extremes of our life, what should be its contours, blur at their point of origin, then disappear into the arms of the Smiling Christ at Forest Lawn. The secretary with the diaphragm in her purse, prepared to meet any emergency, will prove to be a reader of Norman Vincent Peale or Kahlil Gibran. Ten minutes of her luncheon will be turned over to *The Mature Mind*. The raw material world of facts, of *real* personal life, comes full circle in the unreal phantom who spends real time seeking for his or her self in the How-to-do-it Books. How to Live, How to Love, and sooner or later, How to Read Books.

What was once raw about American life has now been dealt with so many times that the material we begin with is itself a fiction, one created by Twain, Eliot, or Fitzgerald. *From Here to Eternity* reminds us that young men are still fighting Hemingway's war. After all, it is the one they know best: it was made real and coherent by his imagination.

Many writers of the twenties, that huge season, would appear to be exceptions to the ravages of raw material, and they are. But it is the nature of this exception to prove the rule. In inspiration, the twenties were singularly un-American. An exile named Pound established its standards, and the left bank of Paris dictated its fashions. This lucid moment of grace was Continental in origin. With the exiles' return, however, it came to an end. The craftsmen who shaped and were shaped by this experience—Eliot, Moore, Fitzgerald, Crane, Hemingway, and so on—maintained their own devotion to the new standards, but they had little effect on the resurgent raw-material school. Whitman's barbaric yawp, which Pound had hoped to educate, reappeared in the gargantuan bellow of Wolfe and a decade of wrath largely concerned with the seamy side of life.

Once again that gratifying hallucination—the great BIG American novel—appeared in cartons too big for the publisher's desk. Once again the author needed help—could one man, singlehanded, tame such a torrent of life? If the writer caged the monster, shouldn't the editor teach him to speak? The point was frequently debated; the editor-collaborator became a part of the creative project, the mastering of the material as exhausting as mastering life itself. In a letter to Fitzgerald, who had suggested that there might be room for a little more selection, Thomas Wolfe replied: "I may be wrong but all I can get out of it is that you think I'd be a better writer if I were an altogether different writer from the writer I am."

Time and the river—was Fitzgerald suggesting they reverse themselves? That a writer swim against the very current of American life? He was, but the suggestion has never been popular. Tom Wolfe didn't take it, and the writer who does take it may find himself, however home-grown, an exile. He swims against the current; and the farther he swims, the more he swims alone. The best American fiction is still *escape* fiction—down the river on a raft, into the hills on a horse, or out of this world on a ship—the Territory ahead lies behind us, safe as the gold at Fort Knox.

IV

Now, raw material, an excess of both material and comparatively raw experience, has been the dominant factor in my own role as a novelist. The thesis I put forward grows out of my experience, and applies to it. Too much crude ore. The hopper of my green and untrained imagination was both nourished and handicapped by it.

Before coming of age—the formative years when the reservoir of raw material was filling—I had led, or rather been led by, half a dozen separate lives. Each life had its own scene, its own milieu; it frequently appeared to have its own beginning and ending, the only connecting tissue being the narrow thread of my *self*. I had been *there*, but that, indeed, explained nothing. In an effort to come to terms with the experience, I processed it in fragments, collecting pieces of the puzzle. In time, a certain over-all pattern *appeared* to be there. But this appearance was essentially a process —an imaginative act of apprehension—rather than a research into the artifacts of my life.

The realization that I had to create coherence, conjure up my synthesis, rather than find it, came to me, as it does to most Americans, disturbingly late. Having sawed out the pieces of my jigsaw puzzle, I was faced with a problem of fitting them together. There is a powerful inclination to leave this chore to someone else. In the work of Malcolm Cowley on William Faulkner, we may have the rudiments of a new procedure. Let the critic do what the author fails to do for himself. As flattering as this concept might be—to both the author and the critic—it must be clear that the concept is not tenable. The final act of coherence is an imaginative act—not a sympathetic disposal of parts—and the man who created the parts must create the whole into which they fit. It is amusing to think what the mind of Henry James would make of this salvage operation, a surgical redistribution of the parts of a patient who is still alive. Mr. Cowley's service to the reader is important—what I want to put in question is his service to the writer. This is implicit, if unstated, in any piece of reconstruction that attempts to implement what the writer failed to do himself.

This act of piety toward the groping artist—a desire to help him with his raw-material burden—is one with our sentiment that he labors to express the inexpressible. Like a fond parent, we supply the words to his stuttering lips. We share with him, as he shares with us, an instinct that our common burden of experience, given a friendly nudging, will speak for itself. At such a moment the mind generates those evocations peculiar to the American scene; life, raw life of such grace that nature seems to be something brought back alive. Out on his raft Huck Finn muses:

Two or three days and nights went by: I reckon I might say they swum by, they slid along so quiet and smooth and lovely. Here is the way we put in the time.

In what follows we are putting in our own time. We are there. Memory is processed by emotion in such a way that life itself seems to be preserved in amber. But we know better; we know that it is more than life, and it is this knowledge that makes it so moving—life has been imagined, immortal life, out of thin air. Not merely that boy out on the river but the nature of the world's imagination, there on the raft with him, will never again be the same. But at the end of his adventures, at the point where the fiction—like the reader—merges into fact, Huck Finn sums it all up in these pregnant words:

But I reckon I got to light out for the Territory ahead of the rest, because Aunt Sally she's going to adopt and civilize me, and I can't stand it. I been there before.

So has the reader. Aunt Sally has his number, but his heart belongs to the Territory ahead.

THE MYTHIC PAST

If we should now ask ourselves what it is that the common and the uncommon American have in common, the man in the street and the sophisticate, the hillbilly and the Ivy Leaguer, I think we have an answer. Nostalgia. This bond joins, in sweet fraternity, such elements as the *Saturday Evening Post* and the *New Yorker*: such artists as Norman Rockwell and E. B. White. It is the past, the mythic past, that is real in Mr. White's lucid prose and Mr. Rockwell's illustrations. The present exists—in so far as it exists—in order to heighten the comparison. Urban sophisticate and cracker-barrel yokel share the oxygen tent of nostalgia. In their commitments to the past Mr. Rockwell and Mr. White—poles apart in technique—process the same sentiments. It is the past that is real. The second tree from the corner is rooted in it. From this commitment Mr. White distills a memorable blend of truth and poetry, leaving to Mr. Rockwell the less memorable elements. But both craftsmen press the same grapes, and bottle the same vintage. They offer us a sweet or dry version of the fictive past.

Mr. White may be right—no writer states his case with more convincing persuasion—but the rightness or the wrongness of his preference is not central to our discussion. What *goes* in his case is what goes without saying in both the *Saturday Evening Post* and the *New Yorker*. That is nostalgia. An implicit, understandable preference for the past.

But there would seem to be a law that the imagination can not deal creatively with secondhand material. What has been done has been done. It resists further tampering. There can be only one Hamlet, one Don Quixote, one Ivan Karamazov, and one Huck Finn, although the world, since nature imitates art, will be peopled with their likenesses.

The mind that falls under the spell of such an artist must exorcise this spell before it can be itself. The possession of the reader is the trap for the writer—he must first fall into it, then escape from it. His affection and admiration for the past—above all for the craft that created such a past—he must express in an imaginative act that blends both piety and cannibalism. In order to begin anew, as André Malraux has pointed out, the artist must cut the ties that bind him.

Every genius leads a revolt against a previous form of possession . . . it is the fact that he alone, amongst all those whom these works of art delight, should seek, by the same token, to destroy them.

Until he does this he cannot process his own reality. The great tradition is not a pious submission to and maintenance of the status quo, but an act of renewal that involves this destructive element.

This goes on—as long as art goes on—before our very eyes. What is currently *raw* in Southern writing derives from the imagination of William Faulkner rather than from the rawness of

Southern life itself. This bondage will persist, these *facts* will seem the real ones, until another writer, with his own spell, removes Faulkner's enchantment to replace it with his own.

In a less dramatic way this has occurred to the country at large. The imagination has now left its stamp on all of it. The names on the land now turn up as the themes or the titles of books. The dry places and the wet, the forces natural and unnatural, have been catalogued. Death Valley offers cocktails and innerspring trail rides to the new generation of pioneers, and the words "dude" and "ranch" are now inseparable. Talent now *originates* in Las Vegas, and the same nylon sweaters, with the same walking shorts, are seen on what appear to be the same teen-agers in Red Wing, Minnesota; Nacogdoches, Texas; and the Bronx. The same popular songs, sung by the same singers, are heard in Seneca, Kansas; Winnemucca, Nevada; or in the car cruising along through what is still described as Donner Pass. Of all questions that face the nation, the $64,000 one is uppermost.

The *region*—the region in the sense that once fed the imagination—is now for sale on the shelf with the maple-sugar Kewpies; the hand-loomed ties and hand-sewn moccasins are now available, along with food and fuel, at regular intervals on our turnpikes. The only regions left are those the artists must imagine. They lie beyond the usual forms of salvage. No matter where we go, in America today, we shall find what we just left.

Raw material, the great variety of it, has been the central ornament of American writing since Thoreau went to Walden, and Whitman took to the open road. The vitality of such material is contagious—it alternately charms and appalls the world—but we have come to the end of what is raw in the material vein. Life, raw life, no longer beckons at the edge of the clearing, to be had for the asking, but must be wooed in the parlor with Aunt Sally as chaperon. Such materials as we have are now attached to her apron strings.

133

In Fitzgerald's *The Great Gatsby*, and I think only in Gatsby, the mythic vastness of this continent, the huge raw material banquet that Wolfe bolted, received its baptismal blessing and its imaginative processing:

And as the moon rose higher the inessential houses began to melt away until gradually I became aware of the old island here that flowered for Dutch sailors' eyes—a fresh, green breast of the new world. Its vanished trees, the trees that made way for Gatsby's house, had once pandered in whispers to the last and greatest of all human dreams; for a transitory enchanted moment man must have held his breath in the presence of this continent, compelled into an esthetic contemplation he neither understood nor desired, face to face for the last time in history with something commensurate to his capacity for wonder.

This is not description but incantation, an evocation of the dream and our capacity for wonder, which found in the dark fields of the republic its mythic equivalent. Nostalgia, perhaps the most inexhaustible of human sentiments, found in this green world of the imagination its permanent refuge, out of time, out of reach, but not out of mind.

II

"Try to be one of the people," Henry James advised the writer, "on whom nothing is lost!" and it was his ironic fate, in being such an artist, to alienate himself from the American reader, on whom his formidable craftsmanship is all but lost. It is neither through subject matter nor taste, but through sheer brilliance of technique that James is exiled from his countrymen. He transformed our raw material to the point where we found it unrecognizable.

In American experience, raw material and nostalgia appear to be different sides of the same coin. The rawer the material, the more nostalgia it evokes—rawness being the hallmark of the real thing, the natural. The classic examples of nostalgia, however, prove to be triumphs of technique: Huck Finn is such a triumph over Tom Sawyer, just as Faulkner is a triumph over Wolfe. And yet the tension that exists between the artist and his material—between the imaginary past and the raw material present —appears to generate what is fresh and distinguished in our writing, from *Winesburg, Ohio*, to *The Adventures of Augie March*.

Privately, in the depths of our being, we are Huck Finns fleeing from Aunt Sally—publicly we create and promote the very civilization we privately reject. With our eyes fixed on the past we walk, blindfolded, into the future. It is little wonder the American mind sometimes wonders where it is going, and what, indeed, it is to be an American. On the evidence we might say it is a man who attempts to face both ways. In the eyes of the world we are the future, but in our own eyes we are the past. Nostalgia rules our hearts while a rhetoric of progress rules our words.

A free man must be free to live where he must, admitting to the compulsions of his nature, in the woods with Thoreau, on a raft with Huck Finn, or sauntering down the Open Road with Whitman. But we forget that Thoreau, a Yankee realist to the marrow, after two years in the woods called off the *experiment. He* called it off, but *we* prefer to think that he is permanently anchored at Walden Pond. That is where his life, as well as his experiment, seems to end for us. His own prevailing tendency was modified by the woody grain of his experience, but in the minds of his countrymen it is still the tendency that remains.

Stock taking, inventory, is the first effort of the mind to make itself at home. We see it in Thoreau—it took him to Walden for both a personal and a Nature stock taking—we see it in the Homeric catalogue and poetic inventory of Whitman. But how does one do it where the home will not stay *put*? Where the stock of items on the shelves changes every day? Whitman did not feel this burden as we do—not until his later years—but he began under an even greater handicap. There was simply too much. The mind staggered under the weight of it. The impulse to get away from it all—as trifling as it may now seem to us—sent Thoreau to Walden and Whitman out on the Open Road. The pattern, however embryonic, is being set up. It is a pattern of flight from a world that will not stand still. The rising tide of cities, and of men, not to mention the appalling flood of objects, forces the man who is aware of these objects into a retreat. It is why we see Tom Wolfe, like a berserk Paul Bunyan, trying to gulp one world and plow under another. It is also why exile has for the American artist a peculiar charm. Somewhere—somewhere *else*, that is—perhaps the world stands still. Perhaps there he can put his thoughts in order—if he has any. But it is raw material that puts him to flight, and as a rule, like Huck Finn, he slips the noose of Aunt Sally and makes for the Territory ahead. That is usually where we find him—if we take the trouble to look for him. Huck Finn is still out on the river, on his raft, drifting through the landscape currently leased to Mr. William Faulkner, but otherwise unchanged. The same natives and Indians still peer at him from the scrub along the shore. The same virtues are being defended, the same changes are being deplored, and the same fears of the future send refugees into the past.

III

In a review of Wolfe's *Letters* Malcolm Cowley observed: "Considering his dependence on what he remembered, Wolfe was lucky that his adolescence, with its intense perceptions, lasted much longer than it does with most writers."

Writer and critic, in this observation, are in common agreement as to what counts. What counts is adolescence, with its intense perceptions, and Wolfe was luckier than most since his adolescence lasted the length of his life. His greatest piece of luck, that is, was that he never grew up. He was Huck Finn Wolfe, out on one raft or another, carried along by Time and the River toward that never-never land of heart's desire, the Territory ahead. He got away from Aunt Sally by growing bigger, but without growing *up*. The dream of adolescence is the giant who remains a boy at heart.

Something in American sentiment and sensibility prefers it that way. We want our raw material raw. We often want it rawer than it actually is. On a practical, day-by-day level this is the preference we have for the man who feels, and the distrust we feel for the man who thinks. It is the root and the flower of the anti-egghead platform in American life. The thinking man, above all the artist whose art transforms a sow's ear into a silk purse, is understandably the enemy of the man who prefers the sow's ear. Anti-eggheadism is not a simple, semi-literate prejudice. It is rooted in a central American presumption that life, raw life, and material, raw material, is superior to the form, the abstraction, that the mind must make of it. The raw material we can get our hands on, the *form* eludes our grasp. Here is where science, applied science, with its conversion of the crude into something refined, something useless into something useful, deeply satisfies the American instinct for the artifact. It is the nature of art to be immaterial, the conceptual act must be grasped by the mind: what appears to be solid is transformed into a vapor thinner than air. That, indeed, is its very indestructibility. Aspirin and barbiturates are factual things, they kill real pain and promote real sleep, but the pain and the lack of sleep arise from invisible fears. Only the laying on of invisible hands will quiet them.

The principle of waste, on which so much of our life and economy seems grounded, is not one that pays off imaginatively. These losses prove to be irreparable. The isolated monuments, the isolated efforts, that characterize the American imagination, symbolize the isolation in which Americans live. Connections are missing. The whole does not add up to something more than the sum of the parts. No synthesizing act of the imagination has as yet transformed us into a nation. We come by our nature *naturally*. We are joined by highways, networks and slogans, not by imaginative acts. Mother's Day, Father's Day and Thanksgiving now join us in a bond of ready-made greetings, double-breasted turkeys, and the queues that form where unwanted holiday gifts are exchanged. The Everyman in America will soon be the one who has Everything.

How did we get this way? By doing—as the song says—what comes naturally. What comes naturally, that is, to us. Mark Twain's preference for life, *real* life, in contrast to such a piece of fiction as Huck Finn, he makes clear in a letter to an unidentified correspondent:

Now then: as the most valuable capital, or culture, or education usable in the building of novels is personal experience, I ought to be well equipped for that trade. I surely have the equipment, a wide culture and all of it real, none of it artificial, for I don't know anything about books.

He knew quite a bit about books, of course, but the nature of the boast is instructive. He felt it was better that he shouldn't. That he had gone to no school but the school of hard knocks. He persuaded himself to believe—in spite of knowing better—that in the building of novels the only equipment a man needed was personal experience, preferably lots of it.

Now personal experience, especially too much of it, actually constitutes an obstacle to the craft of fiction. Too much raw material is as great a hazard as not enough. The hopper of the shaping imagination cannot process too great a load of personal experience. Every publishing season, if not several times a season, we bear witness to this fact. Huge slabs of raw life, the rawer the better, are offered to us. The figure of Tom Wolfe, bolting, in his hunger, more than he could swallow without choking, symbolizes this dilemma but has done little to diminish it. The truth is, the spectacle exhilarates us. Out of Texas a few years ago—and from where else would it come than from out of Texas—came what was modestly described as the biggest novel in the world. Naturally. There was hardly a ripple of surprise. When one reflects that Texas, tremendous as it is, is still only a part of the United States, the problem that faces the American novelist is staggering. Life—all of our lives, that is—is just too big and grand a thing to pin down in a book. It would take a giant to do it—and several giants have tried. One from Minnesota, almost seven feet tall, gave it a try until the public lost interest, and we all know Tom Wolfe's huge grapple with the continent. We all knew—even as Wolfe did—that he would fail. He had to fail in order to prove how BIG we were. He had to fail, since what he set himself to do was impossible. Just the other day William Faulkner, in one of his now frequent interviews, referred to Thomas Wolfe as the greatest American of them all.

Why? Because he tried to do the impossible. The romantic agony could hardly be better phrased. Nor failure so credible and flattering. To fail, that is, is the true hallmark of success.

Coming from Mr. Faulkner this judgment reveals, in all its lush natural disorder, the schizoid soul of the creative American. It tells us more of Mr. Faulkner than meets the eye in his works. Wolfe's verbal bacchanal, a Walpurgisnacht of infinite adolescent yearning and seminal flow, left in its wake a ruin of rhetoric dear to the American heart. A sentimental scene of havoc testifying to the powers of raw American life. In Tom Wolfe was reborn the myth of the native force that would brook no restraint, and we have not yet cleared away the alluvial deposit of his rhetoric. The love that has no appeasement, the quest that has no resolution, the hunger that has no gratification is highly recommended as suitable fare for growing minds. Wolfe's "insatiable appetite for life" is put forward as part of his genius rather than as a disturbing and pitiless form of his impotence. It is in Wolfe's recently published letters that we find the key to his power as a writer. He is an author of confessions—romantic confessions in the manner of Rousseau—and when he is free of the demands of fiction, the problems of creation, he is free to tell us *all*, which is precisely what he does. His chronic incapacity for selection—in confessions *everything* matters—may soon relegate the letters to the limbo of the fiction; but as a writer of confessions his gifts and his torments were in balance. All he had to do, all he wanted to do, was tell us how he *felt*, and in this he succeeded.

But Wolfe's great public success is a measure of the public need. He can best be understood as a martyr to the American greed for life. What we observe in Wolfe is a man eating: a man whose eating does him no good. His books offer us the spectacle of the artist as a cannibal. Life, both literature and life, was something he wanted to devour. How possess, how truly possess, the visible? Wolfe fled this impasse like the hound of heaven; his personal solution was to keep moving, tirelessly tramping up and down the gangplanks of the world. His artistic solution was to write the same book over and over again. Each time in the hope that his self-doubt would stop tormenting him. The one intuition that did not betray him was his haunting sense of artistic failure. The world-wide chorus of praise did not beguile him. He *knew*. As a martyr to our greed, our lust for life that makes life itself an anticlimax, he is such proof as we need that appetite and raw material are not enough.

I have singled out Wolfe because he symbolizes, in his life and in his art, certain native traits, virtues we would call them, carried to the point of self-destruction. An insatiable hunger, an insatiable desire, is not the sign of life but of impotence. Impotence, indeed, is part of the romantic agony. If one desires what one cannot have, if one must do only what cannot be done, the agony in the garden is of self-induced helplessness. It is Wolfe's tragic distinction that he suffered this agony for all of us.

IV

If William Faulkner has become, as there is some reason to believe, a victim of his own transfiguring imagination, he now inhabits a world that is more enduring than the one he left. This new world is compounded, as the old was not, of indestructible elements. Like Henry James, through sheer brilliance of technique Faulkner has transformed his raw material to a point where most of us find it unrecognizable. This shocks us, but we are never led to doubt—as we are with James—that the raw material is still there, since it is the nature of Faulkner's transformation to heighten its apparent *rawness*. It is precisely the rawness of it that has amazed the world. It justifies their conception, derived from our fiction, of a wilderness as yet untamed, a violent land where such goings-on are commonplace. It is apparent to them that Faulkner is also a stylist, but to admit that this world is a product of "technique" would be to say that his books are not *echt* American—not representative, that is, of our eruptive, volcanic life. So they read him as we do, because he is raw, but the spell he has thrown on the world's imagination is a real spell; and, like all real spells, it is pure technique. In his madness, that is, there is method. Here it is at work:

There was a wistaria vine blooming for the second time that summer on a wooden trellis before one window, into which sparrows came now and then in random gusts, making a dry vivid dusty sound before going away: and opposite Quentin, Miss Coldfield in the eternal black which she had worn for forty-three years now, whether for sister, father or nothusband none knew, sitting so bolt upright in the straight hard chair that was so tall for her that her legs hung straight and rigid as if she had iron shinbones and ankles, clear of the floor with that air of impotent and static rage like children's feet, and talking in that grim haggard amazed voice until at last listening would renege and hearing-sense self-confound and the long-dead object of her impotent yet indomitable frustration would appear, as though by outraged recapitulation evoked, quiet inattentive and harmless, out of the biding and dreamy and victorious dust.

This outrage of language, this squeezing on of color, is intended to produce a specific effect. This effect is transformation. The raw material, strictly speaking, has disappeared. What we now have before us is less a scene, *qua* scene, but rather a process. This technique is unusual in literature, but we are familiar with it in paint. Paint *can* be squeezed from the tube, and color *can* be placed beside shrieking color. The expression is the thing. So we call them *Expressionists.** They give expression, in this way, to the pent-up sense of outrage—an *impotent* outrage—that modern life builds up in most of us. Impotent and static rage is at the heart of Faulkner's violence. He tells us this, in a rage of words, repeatedly. The legs of Miss Coldfield, hanging clear of the floor with that impotent and static rage of children's feet—these legs are the conductors of the charge that Faulkner must express. Only such a technique, handled with precision, could discharge such emotion, and generate in the artist the conceptual power to re-create the past.

It is hard to overpraise the charge and revelation this passage carries. Here is the mind of Faulkner's South, an old shell buried in the earth, but one has the feeling that it is about to go off. The heat and summer stillness, the random gusts of sparrows, and Miss Coldfield in her eternal black, all contribute to a scene that totters on the edge of violence. Through Faulkner the mind of the South finds its expression—if not its deliverance. But neither

* I have discussed this technique at some length in the *Magazine of Art*, March, 1952.

142

rage nor outraged recapitulation will revive the long-dead dream of the past, and out of the dreamy victorious dust conjure up for us a convincing present.

But at the opposite pole of Faulkner's impotent rage is his mythic peace. This is the world of Ikkemotubbe, Log-in-the-Creek, and that white man David Hogganbeck, who told the steamboat where to walk. This landscape glows with a softer light, and it is here, in this flowering wilderness, that Faulkner gives free rein to his mythic humor. It has the faculty of both clearing the air and dissolving his rage. There is nothing in the world's literature to compare with the courtship of Hogganbeck and Ikkemotubbe for Hermann Basket's sister, that primal and ever receding vision of womanly loveliness. The green dream that haunted Huck Finn, the green light that forever lured Gatsby, is here enshrined in a glade where corruption will never lay hands on it. We might call it the final resting place of The Territory Ahead. A great Good Place preserved in the grain of the American mind.

If Faulkner wants to tell us this place will endure he has earned the right. Here he no longer speaks for just himself, or Frenchman's Bend, or even time out of mind—here he is the mythic voice of the continent itself. That fresh green breast of the world that once flowered for Fitzgerald—and Dutch sailors' eyes. Here he holds his rage, he is all ears to the voice that panders in such persuasive whispers to the last and greatest of all human dreams. For a transitory moment he holds his wrath in the presence of this voice, this Territory ahead, compelled to a creation he hardly understands, face to face for the last time with something commensurate with his capacity for wonder.

To David Hogganbeck's statement that there is, for all men, just one wisdom, no matter who speaks it, Ikkemotubbe replies: "Aihee. At least, for all men one same heartbreak."

This wisdom has its indestructible elements. Paradise Lost,

never to be regained, still generates in Adam such dreams as he has, and Faulkner testifies to one that is both universal and American. To that extent, who can say that the times have changed? Time present is no different from time past. In that landscape of one same heartbreak, Faulkner has joined hands with the Mournful Knight of Cervantes. With him he has earned the right to remind us that although it is Sancho who inherits the world, it is the Helmet of Mambrino, that illusion, that makes it desirable.

V

When Faulkner tells us that men are indestructible, we are, being men, reassured to hear it, but if we live and have our being in our own time we know that this is not so. The destructive element is inherent in man's very will to create. In atomic fission this fact breaks through the pious clichés associated with creation —any creation—to reveal the risks involved in any truly creative act. In the act, that is, of making anything new. A rhetorical passage will neither redeem man nor save him from himself.

In a series of statements since coming out of retirement, Mr. Faulkner less and less resembles citizen Faulkner, of Oxford, Mississippi, and more and more one of the characters in his books. He invites us to regard him, pen in hand, at the open door of a New Orleans brothel, advising the young writer that the house of ill fame affords ideal conditions for creative work.

This is the voice of a past no longer of use to us. It speaks out again, with echoing remoteness, in and between the lines of his Nobel Prize statement. "I believe that man will not merely endure," he tells us, "he will prevail." These words generate more heat than light. Such light as they do generate illuminates a scene that is far from reassuring, with author Faulkner surrounded by a curious assortment of bedfellows. Thousands who would not, or could not, read his books find this statement of faith wonderfully fortifying. In their minds it amounts to a rejection of his truly creative work. The appeal of the statement seems to lie in the hope that Mr. Faulkner, once a rebel of sorts, has at long last seen the light and returned to the fold, admitting that he believes what we all had the good sense to believe all along.

More convincingly, it seems to me, Mr. Faulkner also spoke of our fear of annihilation, but I believe it is survival—the *wrong* kind of survival—that haunts the mind of the artist. It is not fear of the bomb that paralyzes his will—a fear, that is, that man has no future—but rather a disquieting and numbing apprehension that such future as man has may dispense with art. With *man*, that is, such as we now know him, and such, for all his defects, as art has made him. It is the *nature* of the future, not its extinction, that produces in the artist such foreboding, the prescient chill of heart of a world without consciousness.

This unconscious world grows, all too palpably, out of the manifold tendencies that prevail around him, and the habit of science, applied science, to dispense with the need of art. The artist does not want man merely to prevail, but to prevail as he has been able to conceive him. A more fully conscious, fully sentient being, rather than a less. The survival of men who are strangers to the nature of this conception is a more appalling thought than the extinction of the species. This seeming paradox is at the core of the mind's anxiety. Nor is the survival of such men a fiction, but exists in fact in those men whose brains, as we say, have been washed, or whose tensions have been relieved by the drug or the surgical knife.

AFTER STRANGE GODS

The problem of tradition and the individual talent might be expressed in this way: until the life of literature is equal in importance to the personal life of the writer, his personal life will seldom enter the stream of literature.

If I have emphasized technique, the primacy of technique, over such things as experience and raw material, it is because the primacy of life—in the American scene—is obvious. Such balance as needs redressing is all one way. It is in the interests of such life—the life in literature—that technique is indispensable. Had Proust not *lived* a life, and in his own fashion, his cork-lined chamber would have merely been his coffin, not the crucible where he transmuted such a life as he had lived into art. The primacy of technique is based on the assumption that the raw material is there, not on the anvil, not on the premise that the material itself is conjured out of thin air. What the artist seems to distill from the air is the shape into which the material is forged. But there is no substitute for the material itself—the *life* in literature.

If the modern temper, as distinct from the romantic, lies in the admission that men are mortal, this admission determines the nature of the raw material with which the artist must work. An element of despair, a destructive element, is one of the signs by which we shall know him—the other is the constructive use to which this element is put. It distinguishes this artist from the seriously hopeful, or the hopefully serious, who cannot bring themselves to admit of the contemporary facts. These men *know* better, almost without exception, but their hope lies in the refusal to admit what they know. This common failure of admission characterizes their work and blights their hope. The modern temper finds its facts, and its hope, in the statement by Albert Camus: "I want to know if I can live with what I know and only with that." Nothing could be farther from the bohemian traditions, the irresponsible clichés of the artist's life, than this discipline of facts he must face and master in the name of his art. He must become that paradox, both a visionary and a realist. These are strange Gods to reconcile in one man, and in one art. To what extent does the modern artist succeed—to what extent does he fail? We need representative men, and we have them, in James Joyce, T. S. Eliot and D. H. Lawrence. All men, in their fashion, after strange Gods.

In Joyce's *Portrait of the Artist As a Young Man*, the young man, Stephen Dedalus, makes this confession to his friend Cranly:

You made me confess the fears that I have. But I will tell you also what I do not fear. I do not fear to be alone or to be spurned for another or to leave whatever I have to leave. And I am not afraid to make a mistake, even a great mistake, a lifelong mistake and perhaps as long as eternity too.

In this statement we have the temperament, the devotion, and the prophetic life of the artist. We also have more than a hint that he is after strange Gods. He does not fear to make a mistake: a lasting mistake. We know, now, to what extent Joyce realized this prophecy, although we cannot judge, as yet, to what extent he made a mistake. One of the master craftsmen of literature, not merely of his own time but of any time, in *Finnegans Wake* technique has become an end in itself. Both the life of the artist, and his works, dissolve into it. The admiration we feel for his unexampled devotion should not blind us to the price he paid for it. He stopped living. Like Proust, he began remembering.

Every artist, in his fashion, faces this dilemma—in the name of life he must choose art—but if he gives up living he runs the risk of losing them both. I believe this crisis is dramatized in *Finnegans Wake*. Joyce was left with no alternative to grinding up his own work and starting over, since nothing of importance, except his work, had happened to him. The consequential events of his life were those of his adolescence and young manhood—in his exile, in his withdrawal from Dublin, he withdrew from the world. Dublin *was* his life, and in *Ulysses* he processed it. *Finnegans Wake* is less an example of the inscrutable ways of genius than an instance of genius having run out of raw material. An artist who finds himself, that is, with nothing but his own works on his hands. Through technique Joyce endeavored to make it new. I believe this is why it will largely remain impenetrable. Not because it seems so verbally opaque, but because it conceals so little of interest. With a little probing the reader senses that he has been there. He has *had* it. Little new has been added but the difficulty. In solving the puzzle the reader has solved nothing else. It is the same old Dublin. Only the life has gone out of it.

The keys to. Given. A way a lone a last a loved a long the riverrun past Eve and Adam's, from swerve of shore to bend of bay, brings us by commodius vicus of recirculation back to Howth Castle and Environs.

As, indeed, it does. We have been there before. If Joyce's effort has a meaning to the writer who will never approach him in technique, it lies in the demonstration that technique is not enough. If devotion to his craft deprives a man of living, it will end in depriving him of art.

II

Literature, as distinct from life, finds it easier to come to terms with such a puzzle as *Finnegans Wake* than with the fact that the author exchanged so much of his life to accomplish it. Joyce took this risk with his eyes open, and accepted the consequences. But we are men as well as artists, and if art is to remain a permissible illusion there must continue to be room in it for life. The very life that is so conspicuously absent from *Finnegans Wake*. Those faded ghosts of Villiers de L'Isle-Adam who let their servants do their living for them are not the answer, on the evidence, to either life or art.

The dilemma is an old one: the relationship between literature and life. In American terms the problem has been academic—

life has usually overwhelmed literature—the artist haunted by a sense of failure, but partially consoled by his grip on life. Men seem to be driven into one or the other extremity. On the one hand we have the master craftsman, Joyce, armed with nothing but silence, exile and cunning—on the other we have such a figure as D. H. Lawrence. A man of genius, a novelist and a poet, whose primary concern was not art, but *life*. A man who believed, with a devotion and example equal to that of Joyce, that if life itself could be led to the full art would grow out of it. The purpose of art was to make such life possible. To give up living *for art* would have struck him as a form of madness: one of those tragic delusions, fostered by cant and sophistication, which led men to choose the death in life rather than the life in it. To free men from this deception, to give them life rather than art, made him a poet and a novelist. The Gods of Joyce would have struck him as both strange and false.

With characteristic perception T. S. Eliot was the first to recognize this polarity. In *After Strange Gods* he summed it up in this fashion:

We are not concerned with the author's *beliefs*, but with the orthodoxy of sensibility and with the sense of tradition, our degree of approaching "that region where dwell the vast hosts of the dead." And Lawrence is for my purposes, an almost perfect example of the heretic. And the most ethically orthodox of the more eminent writers of my time is Mr. Joyce.

This statement exhibits Mr. Eliot's talent for coining the rules, as well as the terms, of the game that he chooses to play. That we are *not* concerned with the author's *beliefs*, but only with the orthodoxy of his sensibility, is an observation, to speak charitably, that throws light only on the man who made it. But the distinction he draws, if not the terms, is central to our discussion. Some writers appear to be orthodox, others heretics. Mr. Eliot's purpose, however, is not merely to throw light on this schism, but by this light to read the heretic out of the church. Lawrence is not merely unorthodox. He is dangerous.

In an essay published more than thirty years ago, entitled "The Shame of the Person," Laura Riding lucidly anticipated Mr. Eliot's position, and the new criticism:

> There results what has come to be called criticism. . . . In the end the literary sense comes to be an authority to write which the poet is supposed to receive, through criticism, from the age that he lives in. . . . More and more the poet has been made to conform to literature instead of literature to the poet—literature being the name given by criticism to works inspired or obedient to criticism. Less and less is the poet permitted to rely on personal authority. The very word genius, formerly used to denote the power to intensify a sense of life into a sense of literature, has been boycotted by criticism; not so much because it has become gross and meaningless through sentimentality as because professional literature develops a shame of the person, a snobbism against the personal self-reliance which is the nature of genius.

We shall see, in Mr. Eliot's attack on Lawrence, how profoundly she grasped the critical trend, whose tone was established, naturally, by Mr. Eliot. In "Tradition and the Individual Talent," the latitude that exists in theory is singularly circumscribed in practice—by talent Mr. Eliot does not mean *genius*, if genius does *not* choose to knuckle under. Mr. Eliot allows that Lawrence had *genius*, but since his talent was unorthodox, his genius was little more than a critical embarrassment. The shame of Lawrence's *person*—the very substance of his genius—could hardly be better expressed. Lawrence also suffered, Mr. Eliot informs us, from "a lack not so much of information as of the critical faculties which education should give, and an incapacity for what we ordinarily call thinking."

At another time, and in another place, this statement might have served Mr. Eliot as a definition of genius. But Lawrence *suffers* from it. An incapacity for what is ordinarily called thinking did not destroy him, but made him *suspect*. Mr. Eliot's talent for the destructive comment—I mean the lethal, irrelevant comment—is here displayed at its most masterly. It is the donnish form of "A Genius, but—" of Mr. Aldington. At the thought of Lawrence a kind of panic seems to rock Mr. Eliot's mind. What begins as criticism slips imperceptibly into abuse:

The point is that Lawrence started life wholly free from any restriction of tradition or institution, that he had no guidance except the Inner Light, the most untrustworthy and deceitful guide that ever offered itself to wandering humanity. It was peculiarly so of Lawrence, who does not appear to have been gifted with the faculty of self-criticism, except in flashes, even to the extent of worldly shrewdness.

If we look for the source of what is unreasonable in Mr. Eliot's treatment of Lawrence, we shall find it in a review of *Ulysses*, written at the time of its publication:

In using the myth, in manipulating a continuous parallel between contemporaneity and antiquity, Mr. Joyce is pursuing a method which others must pursue after him. . . . It is simply a way of controlling, of ordering, of giving a shape and a significance to the immense panorama of futility and anarchy which is contemporary history. . . . It is, I seriously believe, a step toward making the modern world possible in art.

This is both analysis and prophecy, since Mr. Eliot, as a poet, has continued to give a shape to the immense panorama of futility by manipulating parallels. Both Joyce and Eliot are masters of the collage. The works of both men sometimes contain more of the past than they do of the present—a relevant fact, since it is *in* the past that both men have lived.

But to make the modern world possible in art is not the same, as Lawrence would have insisted, as making life possible in the modern world. The myths that Mr. Eliot is at such pains to parallel are, almost without exception, not acceptable to Lawrence. They were, indeed, the very things that made living his life all but impossible. He chose, both as an artist and as a man, not to manipulate myths but life itself. It is this that stigmatizes him as a dangerous heretic. He was, in fact, anarchy compounded, which may explain, if not justify, the element of panic in Mr. Eliot's attack that leads him into such unwarranted abuse. Lawrence is the pagan bull run amok in the critics' orderly arrangement of myths.

There is no need to let Lawrence speak for himself, since Mr. Eliot's attack has the merit of doing that for him. It is Lawrence's *defects*, indeed, that make him important to us. In this world—the one in which we must live—the strange Gods of D. H. Lawrence appear to be less strange than those of Mr. Eliot. It is why—as the critic describes them—these defects have the ring of familiar virtues. Lawrence speaks as a *man*, that is, a living man, a fearless and independent man, who attempted to live very much as he wrote. His independence, his stubborn self-reliance, his passionate distaste for cant and humbug—are not merely in the vein but in the very grain of the American mind. It is this grain that shows in the mind and prose of Thoreau:

Be it life or death, we crave only reality. If we are really dying, let us hear the rattle in our throat and feel the cold in our extremities; if we are alive, let us go about our business.

This might have served as an epitaph for Lawrence. It brings us face to face with the paradox that it is Lawrence, the Englishman in exile, who speaks for the brave new world, and Eliot, the American in exile, who speaks for the old. It has been the purpose of this inquiry to explain this paradox. Not merely how it came to pass, but that it was inevitable. In the poet from St. Louis we have the classic example, carried to its ultimate conclusion, of the American artist's tendency to withdraw into the past. To withdraw, that is, from America. His knowledge of the past being what it is, Mr. Eliot has been able to withdraw into it deeper than any of his forerunners or contemporaries. In so far as such a past is useful to us, he speaks for it.

Lawrence speaks—whenever he speaks—with a different voice:

For man, the vast marvel is to be alive. For man, as for flower and beast and bird, the supreme triumph is to be most vividly alive. Whatever the unborn and the dead may know, they cannot know the beauty, the marvel of being alive in the flesh. The dead may look after the afterwards. But the magnificent here and now of life in the flesh is ours, and ours alone, and ours only for a time.

That is a voice in the present. It is the speech of a man alive. It is this voice that recommends his wayward genius to us. It is this man of whom we can say—as Picasso said of Matisse—that he has a sun in his belly. The sun in the belly of Mr. Eliot is a mythic sun. It is a clinker to manipulate: the fire has gone out of it. The man alive in the present is that patient etherized on the table, awaiting burial.

In a statement on the importance of the novel, Lawrence observed that "it can inform and lead into new places the flow of our sympathetic consciousness, and it can lead our sympathy away in recoil from things that are dead."

In this, Henry James, the master of consciousness, would have concurred. It is a question of the death in life, or the life in it. We must deal with both. But we must also exercise a preference. Mr. Eliot speaks for the past—that region where dwell the vast hosts of the dead—Lawrence speaks for the present, that region where dwell the rest of us. In these two men, representative men, irreconcilable attitudes toward life and literature come face to face. Each man, in his fashion, seeks to give a form, a shape of significance, to the immense panorama of futility in which we live. Allowing for the truth in each persuasion, it is Eliot who speaks for what lies behind us, and Lawrence, the heretic, who speaks for the Territory ahead.

In his essay on Massinger T. S. Eliot observes:

> He is not, however, the only man of letters who, at the moment when a new view of life is wanted, has looked at life through the eyes of his predecessors, and only at manners through his own.

This seems to me a just and penetrating estimate of Mr. Eliot's role in modern life and letters. It does nothing to diminish his importance, but explains the nature of his persuasion. He speaks for the past, and it is the past that speaks to most of us. The present is a sight on which we turn our backs and lid our eyes. It will not change its nature through a manipulation of parallels. In the sense that Mr. Eliot is important, D. H. Lawrence is indispensable. He is the breath of life in Mr. Eliot's donnish Pantheon.

III

Life, raw life, the kind we lead every day, whether it leads us into the past or the future, has the curious property of not seeming real *enough*. We have a need, however illusive, for a life that is more real than life. It lies in the imagination. Fiction would seem to be the way it is processed into reality. If this were not so we should have little excuse for art. Life, raw life, would be more than satisfactory in itself. But it seems to be the nature of man to transform—himself, if possible, and then the world around him—and the technique of this transformation is what we call art. When man fails to transform, he loses consciousness, he stops living.

Like Walt Whitman we were there, we saw, and we suffered,

but *where* we were, *what* we saw, and *how* we suffered are a mystery to us until the imagination has given them form. And yet imagination, both talent and imagination, are of little value without conception. They are merely the tools, and it is conception that puts them to use. In the novel it is conceptual power, not style nor sensibility, that indicates genius, since only conception responds to the organic pressures of life. The conceptual act is the most organic act of man. It is this that unites him with the processes of nature, with the nature of life. If man is nature self-conscious, as we have reason to believe, art is his expanding conciousness, and the creative act, in the deepest sense, is his expanding universe.

The essential ingredient to any artist—essential to what is conceptual in his talent—is his freedom to describe what he sees, and what he feels: his freedom to realize, like Cézanne, his sensations. Essential to him, that is, is his freedom to be after strange Gods. It is by their strangeness that he will know them, since he conjured them up. They are, by definition, the Gods that beckon him into the Territory ahead.

To be after strange Gods, then, is the artist's calling: to find and serve them is his proper function. His individual talent, if he has one, will displace an old God with a new one—but the new one will bear an astonishing resemblance to the one it displaced. Tradition, in so far as it is living, lives on in him, and he is powerless to thwart it—but what is dead in tradition, the heavy hand of it, he destroys. In this act of destruction he achieves his freedom as an artist, and what is vital in his art is the tradition that he sustains.

"All I have ever made was for the present and with the hope that it will always remain in the present."

This statement by Picasso goes far to explain why, as he grows old, his art grows young. He speaks to us from the same center of living as the voice of Lawrence. The man who lives in the present—in his own present—lives to that extent in both the past and the future: the man who seeks to live elsewhere, both as an artist and as a man, has deceived himself. This is an old deception. It is one of the crowded provinces of art.

But there is, as Picasso shows us, another kind of art: and as Lawrence reminds us:

. . . there is another kind of poetry: the poetry of that which is at hand: the immediate present. In the immediate present there is no perfection, no consummation, nothing finished. The strands are all flying, quivering, intermingling into the web, the waters shaking the moon.

The artist might well ask how, in such a spinning world as ours, he is to know that he stands in the *present*. There are no pat answers, but there are clues. Since he must live and have his being in a world of clichés, he will know this new world by their absence. He will know it by the fact that he has not been there before. The true Territory ahead is what he must imagine for himself. He will recognize it by its strangeness, the lonely pilgrimage through which he attained it, and through the window of his fiction he will breathe the air of his brave new world. Strange, indeed, will be the Gods found to inhabit it.

Flannery O'Connor
The Fiction Writer and His Country

AMONG THE MANY complaints made about the modern American novelist, the loudest, if not the most intelligent, has been the charge that he is not speaking for his country. A few seasons back an editorial in *Life* magazine asked grandly, "Who speaks for America today?" and was not able to conclude that our novelists, or at least our most gifted ones, did.

The gist of the editorial was that in the last ten years this country had enjoyed an unparalleled prosperity, that it had come nearer to producing a classless society than any other nation and that it was the most powerful country in the world, but that our novelists were writing as if they lived in packing boxes on the edge of the dump while they awaited admission to the poorhouse. Instead of this, the editorial requested that they give us something that really represented this country, and it ended with a very smooth and slick shift into a higher key and demanded further that the novelist show us the redeeming quality of spiritual purpose, for it said that "what is most missing from our hot-house literature" is "the joy of life itself."

This was irritating enough to provoke answers from many novelists and critics, but I do not know that any of those who answered considered the question specifically from the standpoint of the novelist with Christian concerns, who, presumably, would have an interest at least equal to the editors of *Life* in "the redeeming quality of spiritual purpose."

What is such a writer going to take his "country" to be? The word usually used by literary folk in this connection would be "world," but the word "country" will do; in fact, being homely, it will do better, for it suggests more. It suggests everything from the actual countryside that the novelist describes, on, to, and through the peculiar characteristics of his region and his nation, and on, through, and under all of these to his true country, which the writer with Christian convictions will consider to be what is eternal and absolute. This covers considerable territory, and if one were talking of any other kind of writing than the writing of fiction, one would perhaps have to say "countries," but it is the peculiar burden of the fiction writer that he has to make one country do for all and that he has to evoke that one country through the concrete particulars of a life that he can make believable.

This is first of all a matter of vocation, and a vocation is a limiting factor which extends even to the kind of material that the writer is able to apprehend imaginatively. The writer can choose what he writes about but he cannot choose what he is able to make live, and so far as he is concerned a living deformed character is acceptable and a dead whole one is not. The Christian writer particularly will feel that whatever his initial gift is, it comes from

God; and no matter how minor a gift it is, he will not be willing to destroy it by trying to use it outside its proper limits.

The country that the writer is concerned with in the most objective way is, of course, the region that most immediately surrounds him, or simply the country, with its body of manners, that he knows well enough to employ. It's generally suggested that the Southern writer has some advantage here. Most readers these days must be sufficiently sick of hearing about Southern writers and Southern writing and what so many reviewers insist upon calling the "Southern school." No one has ever made plain just what the Southern school is or which writers belong to it. Sometimes, when it is most respectable, it seems to mean the little group of Agrarians that flourished at Vanderbilt in the twenties; but more often the term conjures up an image of Gothic monstrosities and the idea of a preoccupation with everything deformed and grotesque. Most of us are considered, I believe, to be unhappy combinations of Poe and Erskine Caldwell.

At least, however, we are all known to be anguished. The writers of the editorial in question suggest that our anguish is a result of our isolation from the rest of the country. I feel that this would be news to most Southern writers. The anguish that most of us have observed for some time now has been caused not by the fact that the South is alienated from the rest of the country, but by the fact that it is not alienated enough, that every day we are getting more and more like the rest of the country, that we are being forced out, not only of our many sins but of our few virtues. This may be unholy anguish but it is anguish nevertheless.

Manners are of such great consequence to the novelist that any kind will do. Bad manners are better than no manners at all, and because we are losing our customary manners we are probably overly conscious of them; this seems to be a condition that produces writers. In the South there are more amateur authors than there are rivers and streams. In almost every hamlet you'll find at least one lady writing epics in Negro dialect and probably two or three old gentlemen who have impossible historical novels on the way. The woods are full of regional writers, and it is the great horror of every serious Southern writer that he will become one of them.

The writer himself will probably feel that the only way for him to keep from becoming one of them is to examine his conscience and to observe our fierce but fading manners in the light of an ultimate concern; others would say that the way to escape being a regional writer is to widen the region. Don't be a Southern writer; be an American writer. Express this great country—which is enjoying an unparalleled prosperity, which is the strongest nation in the world, and which has almost produced a classless society. How, with all this prosperity and strength and classlessness staring you in the face, can you honestly produce a literature which doesn't make plain the joy of life?

The writer whose position is Christian, and probably also the writer whose position is not, will begin to wonder at this point if there could not be some ugly correlation between our unparalleled prosperity and the stridency of these demands for a literature that shows us the joy of life. He may at least be permitted to ask if these screams for joy would be quite so piercing if joy were really more abundant in our prosperous society.

The Christian writer will feel that in the greatest depth of vision, moral judgment will be implicit and that when we are invited to represent the country according to survey, what we are asked to do is to separate mystery from manners and judgment from vision, in order to produce something a little more palatable to the modern temper. We are asked to form our consciences in the light of statistics, which is to establish the relative as absolute. For many this may be a convenience, since we don't live in an age of settled belief; but it cannot be a convenience, it cannot even be possible, for the writer who is a Catholic. He will feel that any long-continued service to it will produce a soggy, formless, and sentimental literature, one that will provide a sense of spiritual purpose for those who connect the spirit with romanticism and a sense of joy for those who confuse that virtue with satisfaction. The storyteller is concerned with what is; but if what is, is what can be determined by survey, then the disciples of Dr. Kinsey and Dr. Gallup are sufficient for the day thereof.

In the greatest fiction, the writer's moral sense coincides with his dramatic sense, and I see no way for it to do this unless his moral judgment is part of the very act of seeing, and he is free to use it. I have heard it said that belief in Christian dogma is a hindrance to the writer, but I myself have found nothing further from the truth. Actually, it frees the storyteller to observe. It is not a set of rules which fixes what he sees in the world. It affects his writing primarily by guaranteeing his respect for mystery.

In the introduction to a collection of his stories called *Rotting Hill*, Wyndham Lewis has written, "If I write about a hill that is rotting, it is because I despise rot." The general accusation passed against writers now is that they write about rot because they love it. Some do, and their works may betray them, but it is impossible not to believe that some write about rot because they see it and recognize it for what it is.

It may well be asked, however, why so much of our literature is apparently lacking in a sense of spiritual purpose and in the joy of life, and if stories lacking such are actually credible. The only conscience I have to examine in this matter is my own, and when I look at stories I have written I find that they are, for the most part, about people who are poor, who are afflicted in both mind and body, who have little—or at best a distorted—sense of spiritual purpose, and whose actions do not apparently give the reader a great assurance of the joy of life.

161

Yet how is this? For I am no disbeliever in spiritual purpose and no vague believer. I see from the standpoint of Christian orthodoxy. This means that for me the meaning of life is centered in our Redemption by Christ and that what I see in the world I see in its relation to that. I don't think that this is a position that can be taken halfway or one that is particularly easy in these times to make transparent in fiction.

Some may blame preoccupation with the grotesque on the fact that here we have a Southern writer and that this is just the type of imagination that Southern life fosters. I have written several stories which did not seem to me to have any grotesque characters in them at all, but which have immediately been labeled grotesque by non-Southern readers. I find it hard to believe that what is observable behavior in one section can be entirely without parallel in another. At least, of late, Southern writers have had the opportunity of pointing out that none of us invented Elvis Presley and that that youth is himself probably less an occasion for concern than his popularity, which is not restricted to the Southern part of the country. The problem may well become one of finding something that is *not* grotesque and of deciding what standards we would use in looking.

My own feeling is that writers who see by the light of their Christian faith will have, in these times, the sharpest eyes for the grotesque, for the perverse, and for the unacceptable. In some cases, these writers may be unconsciously infected with the Manichaean spirit of the times and suffer the much discussed disjunction between sensibility and belief, but I think that more often the reason for this attention to the perverse is the difference between their beliefs and the beliefs of their audience. Redemption is meaningless unless there is cause for it in the actual life we live, and for the last few centuries there has been operating in our culture the secular belief that there is no such cause.

The novelist with Christian concerns will find in modern life distortions which are repugnant to him, and his problem will be to make these appear as distortions to an audience which is used to seeing them as natural; and he may well be forced to take ever more violent means to get his vision across to this hostile audience. When you can assume that your audience holds the same beliefs you do, you can relax a little and use more normal ways of talking to it; when you have to assume that it does not, then you have to make your vision apparent by shock—to the hard of hearing you shout, and for the almost blind you draw large and startling figures.

Unless we are willing to accept our artists as they are, the answer to the question, "Who speaks for America today?" will have to be: the advertising agencies. They are entirely capable of showing us our unparalleled prosperity and our almost classless society, and no one has ever accused them of not being affirmative. Where the artist is still trusted, he will not be looked to for assurance. Those who believe that art proceeds from a healthy, and not from a diseased, faculty of the mind will take what he shows them as a revelation, not of what we ought to be but of what we are at a given time and under given circumstances; that is, as a limited revelation but a revelation nevertheless.

When we talk about the writer's country we are liable to forget that no matter what particular country it is, it is inside as well as outside him. Art requires a delicate adjustment of the outer and inner worlds in such a way that, without changing their nature, they can be seen through each other. To know oneself is to know one's region. It is also to know the world, and it is also, paradoxically, a form of exile from that world. The writer's value is lost, both to himself and to his country, as soon as he ceases to see that country as a part of himself, and to know oneself is, above all, to know what one lacks. It is to measure oneself against Truth, and not the other way around. The first product of self-knowledge is humility, and this is not a virtue conspicuous in any national character.

St. Cyril of Jerusalem, in instructing catechumens, wrote: "The dragon sits by the side of the road, watching those who pass. Beware lest he devour you. We go to the Father of Souls, but it is necessary to pass by the dragon." No matter what form the dragon may take, it is of this mysterious passage past him, or into his jaws, that stories of any depth will always be concerned to tell, and this being the case, it requires considerable courage at any time, in any country, not to turn away from the storyteller.

Harvey Swados
The Image in the Mirror

> May fiction not find a second wind, or a fiftieth, in the very
> portrayal of that collapse? Till the world is an unpeopled void
> there will be an image in the mirror.
> —HENRY JAMES, *The Future of the Novel*

THE PAGES that follow are an appeal to the intelligent reader, whoever he may be, to put aside the
prejudices about the American novel that he has been accumulating over the years, fortified, perhaps even inspired, by the critical
pronouncements of his favorite journals. What I propose he accept
in their place is at least a willingness to grant the hospitality of his
hearth to the American novelist, with all his reputed eccentricity,
tediousness, feebleness and senility; and if what I am going to say
has any validity, he will hopefully find not only that American
literary productivity is considerably less abysmal than he has been
led to believe, but also that the contemporary novelist still has the

power to speak to him, to touch his heart, to open for him, even in his own house, doors the keys to which he thought had been lost and which could not be forced by other locksmiths. In his turn he may discover that if all too many current novels' insights seem devoid of centrality or indeed of any significant relationship to his own inner life, this may not be due unqualifiedly to the willfulness of the novelist, but in some measure to the situation of that novelist, to the critical hostility which greets not the end product alone, but even the presumptuous act of creation, and finally to the indifference of the general public, himself included, toward the problems of the novelist.

It is not without significance that some of the severest fire with which the novelist has been raked comes from just those quarters where one would expect to find, if not a last-ditch defense of the artist, certainly a receptivity to his work in a time of more than ordinary confusion and difficulty. Naturally both the novelist and the intelligent reader whom he presumes to be waiting somewhere as his putative audience are taken aback by this phenomenon: the novelist can only begin to wonder where his friends are and whether they really exist, the reader to wonder whether he is not a fool for caring at all about what is in the new books that are still (despite everything) being published, when it would be so much less demanding to turn to the consolations of the popular entertainments. Since it is my contention that the current attack on the American novel is based on false premises and faulty reasoning, I shall have to devote more space in the following paragraphs to a consideration of its expression in certain periodicals than might otherwise be considered profitable.

In the Summer, 1956, number of *Partisan Review*, Mr. Steven Marcus concludes an appreciation of Evelyn Waugh with some observations on "why writers in America have shown so little capacity for development. It is a truism of our culture that the majority of serious American novelists are 'one book' writers; they either write one large good book and then almost nothing else, or spend their careers writing the same book over and over again. . . . What we sense in the typical American 'giants' who fail, is an enormous talent that is dying unexpressed, a latent richness that can find no means of articulating itself. We regularly produce novelists who seem just on the point of writing really first-class works, while what we get from them are large, unwieldy failures, evidences of an inability to harness or express themselves with any kind of grace or economy. . . . Until the conventions of the written language have become more accessible to our daily speech, America will continue to present us with writers who, though of the highest talents and intentions, are largely brilliant and inspired amateurs. . . ."

Let us pass over the question of why an essay in praise of the virtues of an admittedly minor English novelist should conclude with two pages devoted to minimizing the virtues of admittedly major American novelists. Let us pass over Mr. Marcus's apparent unawareness that the problem of life-long fecundity versus repetitiveness or early silence—crudely, Titian versus Rimbaud—is not merely a shorthand way of contrasting European fertility and American sterility but is an unsolved and perhaps insoluble problem in the relation of artistic productivity to psychic energy, still puzzling critics, historians and psychiatrists. Let us even pass without comment the question of taste involved in mentioning by name such writers as William Faulkner, Mary McCarthy, Thomas Wolfe, Robert Penn Warren and Saul Bellow just prior to the above-quoted lines, with no attempt to document the attack or to remove the implication that at least some of them are "one-book" writers, "failures," or "amateurs." Let us note rather that as we turn the page of the magazine we come immediately upon another assault on the novelist, this time in what purports to be a review of current fiction by Leslie Fiedler, which opens like a direct extension of Mr. Marcus's closing remarks, and which I should like therefore to examine in some detail.

"To read a group of novels is these days a depressing experience. . . . after the fourth or fifth, I find myself beginning to think about 'The Novel,' and I feel a desperate desire to sneak out to a movie." In its fashionableness this complaint is characteristic of a certain group now busily proclaiming to all who will listen its disaffection and disappointment with the modern novel. Mr. Fiedler is depressed by the novel because (1) it is "respectable" and "predictable"; (2) "the consumption of novels has become a dull public observance like going to church"; (3) "the *avant-garde* novel has become a tradition"; (4) "the novel of the last twenty years remains largely sterile" and "there has been no general sense of a new breakthrough"; (5) "the First Novel has become so rigid and conventional in form that it seems an icon."

By his own testimony, Mr. Fiedler belongs to what Henry James called "the group of the formerly subject, but now estranged, the deceived and bored, those for whom the whole movement too decidedly fails to live up to its possibilities. There are people," James went on to add, "who have loved the novel, but who actually find themselves drowned in its verbiage, and for whom, even in some of its approved manifestations, it has become a terror they exert every ingenuity, every hypocrisy, to evade."

If James could render such judgment at the turn of the century, what would he say today, after the great novelists of the fifty years succeeding him have told us at least as much about ourselves and our world as any comparable international body of philosophers or social scientists? Those who turn from the novel for Mr. Fiedler's reasons are exerting more than hypocrisy; they are actuated by precisely that "deep-seated contempt for literature" with which Granville Hicks has sternly but I believe justly charged Anthony West, book reviewer for the *New Yorker*.

Mr. Fiedler assures us that he admires the achievements of the twentieth century masters, that indeed what he is objecting to is that "our novelists in general fight the old fights" and that the contemporary first novel is dismaying "by its bondage to the accidents of biography, its exploitation of the tenderness the young feel toward themselves, its dissolution of form into feeling." But this sighing over a falling-off is nothing more than the stock response of those who always oppose the trivia of the present to the glories of the past, those who assure us that they were, like the hypocrites of James's day, formerly subject, but are now estranged.

The crude conception of culture as consisting simply of a chain of triumphant *avant-garde* masterworks, and the consequent conception of the critic's task implicit in Mr. Fiedler's remarks, rings strangely in the columns of a literary review that has earned a reputation both for seriousness and for literary hospitality. For Mr. Fiedler what lies below the peaks is fit only to be ridiculed because the old fights are still being fought, or haughtily ignored: "I have decided not even to discuss any of the current first novels."

It seems never to have occurred to him that, as André Gide put it, "if there were no names in the history of art except those belonging to the creators of new forms there would be no culture. The very word implies a continuity, and therefore it calls for disciples, imitators and followers to make a living chain; in other words, a tradition."

If Gide's words are true, does it not follow that one of the primary responsibilities of the critical intelligence should be the conscientious examination of the living chain? This entails not simply a bibliographical listing of the new novels, but a consideration without superciliousness or patronizing of what is being done that is most interesting by the disciples, imitators, and followers—if it is true that no one else is producing anything worthy of note. It would seem an elementary rule of critical conduct that one not make unfulfillable claims on what one examines; the critic who approaches the work of others with venom and envy rather than with love and devotion (not necessarily for the work under discussion, but for the culture of which it is a tiny link) is not only going to be unable to infect us with the enthusiasm which should arise from the discovery of a moving artistic achievement; he is going to be unable to tell us precisely why a new work is overvalued or valueless, because inevitably he will confuse his own passion for fashion with a historical sense of the continuity of culture.

Harold Rosenberg put the matter succinctly enough when he wrote (in *Art News*, February, 1956), "Admiring inherited masterpieces in order to saddle contemporaries with the responsibility to equal them is a trick of totalitarians and busybodies." The statement is applicable to book reviewers, even though Mr. Rosenberg was writing about the situation in painting, and was concerned with the attacks on contemporary painting by vulgarians in Congress and in other seats of power and influence, and even though the novelist, unlike the painter, has not been the object of congressional attack, nor has the exportation of his work been questioned by Presidents or State Department officials or envious fellow craftsmen working in an earlier, more conservative tradition.

Perhaps it would have been simpler if the attack on the novelist *had* come primarily from such quarters rather than from within the ranks of his "friends," for then the novelist would at least have felt that he could call upon his allies to support him in a battle for cultural freedom—instead of discovering that the bricks heaved at his head come from those who continue to protest that they love him most. Nevertheless it remains his responsibility to identify and dissociate himself from the totalitarians and busybodies who would prescribe for him, whether their voices are raised in the *Congressional Record*, the *New Yorker*, the *New York Times Book Review*, or the quarterlies.

But when we examine the stylish attitude toward fiction expressed in Mr. Fiedler's essay, we cannot merely reject his strange conception of the critic's function. I would submit also that what he has to say specifically about the recent first novel in America is quite simply not so.

We have heard before the charge that our writers were obsessed in their first novels with formless, overemotional, sentimentalized autobiographical material, and if we look back at the period when many young writers, reacting against the proletarian formula, embraced the mood of Thomas Wolfe, we should have to agree that there was a time when there was a basis to such a charge. But for a supposedly serious critic to make such a statement in 1956 betrays either ignorance or the kind of malice with which noisy ignoramuses attack abstract art by characterizing it as indistinguishable from children's and lunatics' scrawls.

I have myself done considerable reviewing of fiction, and can recall without difficulty a substantial group of first novels of the past few years which were in no way sentimental portraits of the artists as young men. In no particular order, I should list Herbert Gold's *Birth of a Hero*, about a middle-aged Cleveland businessman; William Styron's *Lie Down in Darkness*, chronicle of a Southern family; A. M. Klein's *The Second Scroll*, allegorical drama of Jewish exile and fulfillment; Stephen Becker's *The Season of the Stranger*, a picture of China in transition; Ernst Pawel's *The Island in Time*, a study of Jews in an Italian DP camp; Bernard Malamud's *The Natural*, mythical saga of a baseball hero; James Baldwin's *Go Tell It on the Mountain*, the story of a Negro family seen through a poet's eyes; William Gaddis's *The Recognitions*, a symbolic panorama of counterfeiting in the worlds of art, money, and religion.

And those are only books which I myself have reviewed for

various publications. Readers who follow the course of the novel with any degree of attentiveness can of course add to the list at some length: Ralph Ellison's *Invisible Man*, the adventures of a Negro in a real and unreal world; David Wagoner's *A Man in the Middle*, whose hero is a middle-aged railroad man; my own *Out Went the Candle*, about a wartime profiteer and his relations with his children; N. Martin Kramer's *The Hearth and the Strangeness*, zigzag chronicle of a disturbed family; Sam Astrachan's *An End to Dying* and Adele Wiseman's *The Sacrifice*, both unusually conceived sagas of Jewish immigrant life; and many others.

No one would claim that these first novels are all extraordinary (although certainly two or three of them are just that), that they are all of equal merit, or that they are sure to be read fifty years from now. What can be said is that for one reason or another they stand out from the ordinary, and that in not one case do they correspond in intention or execution to the absurd conception of the American first novel as an adolescent portrait of adolescence. They move in space from the Orient to the Middle East, in characterization from the Chinese peasant to the American businessman to the Israeli pioneer, in style from neo-realistic to fanciful to frankly experimental, in tone and temper from passionately affirmative to unyieldingly pessimistic. Their very existence in print casts an interesting light on Mr. Fiedler's solemn warning that "if one is looking for even the hint of something new, he must avoid the First Novel."

Staring at himself through Mr. Marcus's spectacles, the novelist sees himself as the endless experimenter, hopelessly attempting to achieve compression, grace and facility in a language that is not really his; turning to squint through Mr. Fiedler's bifocals, he sees himself alternatively as a traditional teller of dull tales, or as a second-rater feebly imitating the innovations of his predecessors.

While with one hand Mr. Fiedler deplores the undocumented

prevalence in the first novel of gratuitous autobiographical data, with the other he submits to the readers of *Perspectives USA* his own autobiography. (This is in an article *about Partisan Review*, and the curriculum vitae is presented as the credentials of a more or less typical *Partisan Review* reader and/or contributor). He tells us that he is Jewish, an ex-Trotskyite, a professor of English, and the father of six children. He does not tell us that he is writing—although the inference seems likely—a novel—not, Heaven forbid, a first novel, but a novel nevertheless; nor does he tell us how he would react if and when his own book were published and went unnoticed in *Partisan Review* because its book reviewer took nose between thumb and forefinger at the very sight of a pile of new novels and hurried out instead to his neighborhood movie house.

What I have said thus far has been intended primarily not as an attack on Leslie Fiedler, but rather as a criticism of the mood of which I think he is not unrepresentative and as an examination of the kind of writing about novels that is currently all too common. Of course, it is always tempting to think that it was not ever thus, that there was a time when book reviewing and literary criticism stood in a somewhat closer relationship, just as book reviewers think back nostalgically on a non-existent time when much of what was published was new and exciting and little of what was published was dull and worthless.

But if Henry James conceded in 1900 that fiction "has been vulgarized, like all other kinds of literature, like everything else today, and it has proved more than some kinds accessible to vulgarization," if he asserted that "the high prosperity of fiction has marched, very directly, with another 'sign of the times,' the demoralization, the vulgarization of literature in general, the increasing familiarity of all such methods of communication, the making itself supremely felt, as it were, of the presence of the ladies and children—by whom I mean, in other words, the reader irreflective and uncritical," he also wrote about criticism: "The review is in nine cases out of ten an effort of intelligence as undeveloped as the ineptitude over which it fumbles. . . ."

This is not merely to say that the more things change, the more they remain the same, but to indicate that present problems are not always unique but can often be seen as grotesquely magnified versions of older problems. Fifty years and fifty million tons of paper pulp after James's comment, concurrently with the remarkable discovery of a new public for good novels in cheap reprint editions, there *is* a certain weariness with the novel among the formerly subject, now estranged; and if the disillusioned are not all turning to the movies (the disconsolate captains of Hollywood surely wish that it were so), it may be that they are turning to television, inspirational texts or personal gossip for the values and satisfactions formerly obtained, supposedly, from the novel. We do know that in recent years, even while new thousands have been eagerly buying everything from Faulkner to Spillane in paper covers, the published total of hard-cover fiction titles has been diminishing; we do know that the sales of these titles, even while paperback fiction proliferates, have hardly risen in proportion to the zooming population curves.

Why? Has the writer really failed the reader?

I do not think so. Since the turn of the century mankind has been subjected to a series of cataclysmic shocks unparalleled since the great plagues. It has been tricked and trampled by totalitarian tyrants. It has been dragged into a series of catastrophic wars which have dwarfed in their destructiveness and annihilation the combined effects of all previous military adventures, and which have culminated in the planned and methodical murder of some six million human beings. Obviously the novelist has now to deal with the human heart pushed to such extremities as would have been beyond the most horrid imaginings of a Jane Austen or an Anthony Trollope, or even a Henry James. Can we honestly charge that the novelist has funked his obligation, or that he has utterly failed in its execution? It seems to me that in comparison with what the poet and the playwright have managed to say about the twentieth century world, the novelist comes off very well.

I must confess that I am baffled by V. S. Pritchett's assertion that novelists "have not observed and defined a characteristic man of these years." If he means a characteristic Nazi, one might perhaps agree. But who has told us more about the characteristic Italian peasant, the characteristic Spanish peasant, the characteristic Russian communist, the characteristic American expatriate, than Ignazio Silone, Ralph Bates, Victor Serge, Ernest Hemingway? Can we not say that we have learned as much of what we know of twentieth century man from the novelist as from any other single source, historic or scientific? And if we have suddenly stopped learning about post-Hiroshima, post-Dachau man, may it not be for reasons other than a sudden inexplicable failure of the novelist to come to terms with his world?

Presumably Mr. Pritchett is referring mainly to British and American novelists of the postwar years. Without involving ourselves in the cisatlantic literary scene, we may point out that novelists like Wright Morris have been doing as much to present us with a gallery of characteristic Americans as have any other creative artists on the American landscape. Without claiming that Wright Morris is a supremely gifted innovator, we can say that he has a unique vision of American life and of the American character which is in the nature of a pleasurable revelation. If he goes virtually unread in the United States today, after having published ten or eleven books, this can hardly be laid solely to his own inadequacies, but must be a function of (*a*) the attitude of the reading public, (*b*) the failure of the critic in an age of criticism, and (*c*) the topsy-turvy situation in the publishing business.

A public which ignores a novelist like Wright Morris in favor of its drive-ins or its television screens is hardly in a solid position to protest that its writers are giving it nothing nourishing to feed on. We are not yet faced with a situation like that which prevailed in Russia under Stalin, wherein all writers but the foulest sycophants were silenced, wherein those capable writers who remained at large had to devote themselves to translating the classics, wherein the public turned in disgust from the trash authorized by the régime to the great writers of the past. The American public is not turning from officially sponsored "affirmative" propaganda to the great voices of the nineteenth century; it is turning from—or passing by—the Wright Morrises in favor of the Paddy Chayefskys.

The reading public, much of it "new" and consequently self-conscious, is being ill served by even the most "advanced" critics. (I have no intention here of discussing the New Critics, who are often either determinedly soporific or unintentionally comical, and who in any case rarely stoop—with honorable exceptions—to the textual examination of current fiction.) We know that the readers of the nineteenth century were mostly leisure-class ladies, many of them producers as well as consumers of fiction. We know that these ladies are still the backbone of the book clubs and the circulating libraries; in short, that they are still the principal steady buyers of novels, although they are being joined each year by increasing thousands of young college graduates of both sexes anxious to keep up with what is new and thus be considered in some sense as intellectuals (these are apparently the big new market for paper-cover novels, about which I shall have something to say a little later).

The new novel-reading public grows daily more sophisticated. Yet this is not always to the good, for, since like most new audiences it is unsure of its developing tastes, it tends to turn for guidance to those book reviewers who express their supposed sophistication, like the *New Yorker*'s stable of reviewers, by parading their own erudition and unintentionally revealing the depth of their own contempt for the novel and for what it sets out to do. The review of current fiction which I am afraid I have already treated at unpardonable length concludes, after some highly unflattering remarks about John Hersey and Nelson Algren, with a favorable notice of a new novel by Iris Murdoch, young English writer. The tone of the favorable comment is so guarded and *dispirited* in contrast to the vigor with which Hersey and Algren are demolished that one may legitimately doubt whether a single reader will remember the name of Miss Murdoch's novel—much less be set aflame to read it or—horror of horrors—to buy it.

Those few critics who, like Alfred Kazin and Granville Hicks, are secure enough in their own taste to be able to praise a *new* book (the woods are full of critics who know how to appreciate *old* books, particularly when the authors are dead and incapable of disrupting considered judgments by bringing out something else) without communicating a feeling of acute embarrassment and unease are unfortunately rare indeed. As an example I would point to Mr. Kazin's brief but highly laudatory review in the *New Republic* of J. F. Powers's collected stories: I mention this particular review precisely because, in addition to the fact that I am not always an admirer of this critic's manner, I do not share his enthusiasm for the work of Mr. Powers. Nevertheless Mr. Kazin's intensity of feeling and his generous warmth moved me to reexamine my own response to the Powers stories; had I not already read them, the review would certainly have impelled me to do so. In short, Mr. Kazin was here exercising one of the basic functions of the critic of fiction, one currently ignored when it is not scorned.

"When a literary journalist comes upon a good novel," Granville Hicks commented recently in reviewing Miss Wiseman's *The Sacrifice* for the *New Leader*, "his first obligation is to say so. Afterward he can try to explain why it is good and, if he sees fit, why it is not so good as it conceivably might be. These are important matters, but they are not so important as that an act of creation has taken place."

If the book reviewers for such magazines as the *New Yorker* and the *Partisan Review* think it vulgar to betray enthusiasm even for those few novels of which they approve, can we really expect their readers to step out in advance of them? Those readers are aware that *Marjorie Morningstar*, for example, does not advance their understanding of themselves or their contemporaries —but instead of moving from Mr. Herman Wouk to other novelists who are digging deeper and coming up with purer ore they dismiss the medium as moribund or obsolete, fortified by the obiter dicta of the reviewers. Can it be that this audience's very desires are ambiguous, that even while it eagerly absorbs the more easily assimilable products of our culture, as purveyed by slick-paper weeklies and book clubs, that major portion of it which is mass-oriented nervously rejects without examination those more searching statements of the individual mind because it senses that the best-written and least-sold novels of recent years would raise questions of identity and purpose upon which it is unprepared and unwilling to reflect in the fat years of the fifties?

In any case, we can observe the spectacle of more than one very young man "going into" literary criticism as years ago they would have gone into medicine or law. Seeking quick access to the attention of the new audience, they direct all of their newly acquired vocabulary of invective and derision at those novels whose merits they are, if not blind to, firmly determined to ignore. They have learned that critical names are made not by praise, not even by judicious appreciation, but more commonly by hatchet jobs on the work of their betters.

"In a world in which criticism is acute and mature," wrote Henry James, ". . . talent will find itself trained, in order successfully to assert itself, to many more kinds of precautionary expertness than in a society in which the art I have named holds an inferior place or makes a sorry figure. A community addicted to reflection and fond of ideas will try experiments with the 'story' that will be left untried in a community mainly devoted to traveling and shooting, to pushing trade and playing football." One is tempted to add that talent will not find itself trained, nor public taste elevated, by careerists who treat literary criticism as another means of pushing trade.

As I have indicated, I do not think that the novelist's external problems end with an uncultivated and unreceptive public and a body of venomous or disappointed men serving as his critics. There is also the situation in the publishing world, so ludicrously stacked against the writer that one may marvel that there are still young men and women with the temerity to write and submit first novels. The publisher tells us that he *must* charge four and five dollars for a novel because of his economic position, that the novel today must sell from five to ten thousand copies if it is to show any profit at all, and that it is becoming increasingly more difficult to publish a novel with a predictably smaller market. But he does not tell us where there is to be found a steady market of ten thousand Americans who will spend four or five dollars at frequent intervals for the best fiction he can find to publish.

The position of the New York publisher is becoming more and more like that of the Broadway producer. He is gambling on smash hits, and he can less and less afford to take chances on a newcomer whose work is merely promising, or is more than promising but less than commercial. What is more, in many cases he is frightfully sorry, but he can no longer afford the luxury of carrying on his list a writer who—no matter how highly regarded he may be by critics, editors and a small but faithful body of readers—does not make money for the firm. He can still publish, as a gamble or an investment, a prestige book by a promising new writer; but that new writer's next book had better give proof that it shows some understanding of the requirements of the larger literary market, or in all likelihood it will be politely but firmly rejected.

The effect on the American playwright of this unrealistic cost-price situation (un-American in that it bears more resemblance to the French cartels' archaic underproduction and overpricing of refrigerators than it does to American business practice in other fields) is already painfully apparent. Except for one or two Big Names, who are still almost as much box-office draws as the Hollywood stars regularly co-opted to help ensure Broadway success for their new shows, the American playwright is now little more than a minor member of a collective, endeavoring to manufacture a product salable to the largest possible public; his function may be compared to that of the speech writer or idea man on the team of the campaigning politician. By the time directors, producers and play doctors have finished processing his work, he is only a name in small print on the advance advertising, to be dropped and all but forgotten during the run of the play.

This can hardly be predicted as the inevitable fate of the novelist. But surely the pressure on him to create a marketable product acceptable to those on whom the publisher is increasingly dependent, the book-club and reprint firms, if not the Hollywood producers, is bound to increase. Just as the young dramatist nowadays bends himself to the task of pleasing not himself but the grimly harried real-estate manipulators who may award him an option, so the apprentice novelist, faced with the choice of publication or oblivion, may very well tend to adapt and adjust himself by gradual stages to the needs of his publisher and to what that publisher assures him are the tastes of the waiting public. After all, is he not currently assured from all sides that commercial success and literary achievement are no longer mutually exclusive, but positively complementary in this "affirmative" age?

The publisher who perceives and perhaps fosters the emerging parallel between his speculative endeavors and those of the Broadway producer may not stop to think that the unrealistic economic state of the theater, unlike that of the publishing world, is underpinned by one of the peculiarities of our tax structure. The double factors of the expense account and the entertainment allowance actually represent a concealed federal subsidy of the preposterous Broadway ticket system in which fifty or seventy-five dollars is gladly paid for a ticket to a hit musical show because "nobody" is actually paying such a preposterous price out of his own pocket. According to *Fortune* magazine, between 30 and 40 per cent of all theater seats are sold to expense-account customers. There has not yet been a comparable generosity on the part of the Internal Revenue Bureau toward fiction consumers, nor has anyone yet even claimed a deduction for his annual expenditure on novels, so publishers cannot, like producers, count on the cushion of an assured minimum of expense-account customers.

While doubling the price of their product, they have not doubled their authors' royalties. They cannot afford either, so the story goes, to pay substantial salaries to their younger editors. Although this does not result in their having to make do with inferior help—apparently there is always an adequate supply of young men of private means and of young ladies from female colleges for whom the glamour of the publishing world is an adequate substitute for a living wage—it does effectively close off for most writers an avenue of comparatively undemanding employment that was formerly frequently utilized by writers on their way up.

Caught in the inflationary squeeze, the writer whose books do not sell at least partly because they are priced too high, who cannot support a family in New York City on the salaries paid by publishers, who no longer finds a low-cost bohemia or indeed any interstices of a daily more highly organized society in which he can nest, is being pushed into the college towns in increasing numbers as, we are told, his British cousin has been forced into the employment of the BBC. There has been a good deal of worried discussion about this recently, to which I hesitate to add, but which is so intimately bound up with the current situation of the novelist that I cannot pass it by without comment.

Some of the complaints that security-minded writers are fastening themselves like barnacles to university faculties come from people who are themselves attached to universities or who have private means, and who seem genuinely perturbed that writers who have in the past lived as splendidly enviable bohemians are now concerned with such vulgar problems as making both ends meet. Their perturbation has not as yet taken such a constructive turn as the issuance of suggestions for the solution of these problems without resort to the consolations of college salary checks and their concomitant insurance and pension funds, tenure and long vacations. What is more, the fear that writers who have been drifting back to the campus will cut themselves off from the main currents of American life would appear singularly inappropriate when measured against the background of the writers: depression, war, world-wide cataclysms often lived through at first hand. Those writers who have lived in the world for the last thirty or forty years need have no shortage of usable experience for their individual undertakings, no matter how they earn their livings.

But there is a situation in which these fears for the insulation and isolation of the American writer do have a good deal of point. We do see now the beginnings of a trend which can only be reinforced by the economic factors already touched on. A good many young men who are determined to become writers are already going directly from college to graduate school, from graduate school to teaching and writing, in many cases without ever discovering at first hand the existence of any world other than the academic—with the occasional exception of a European Fulbright year, and that all too often lived through in a little American community scarcely distinguishable from the college town back home. They seem not merely content at spending their lives in such a predictable manner, but terrified at the idea of spending them in any less predictable manner (if envious of those who do somehow manage to). The cult of experience, so castigated as one of the literary fallacies of the thirties, is apparently being replaced in the fifties by the cult of inexperience.

A sheltered existence, from undergraduate adolescence to emeritus retirement, may be a matter of indifference (or indeed of positive benefit) to lecturers in topology or medieval history; to storytellers, romancers, writers of novels, may it not prove disastrous?

We are not speaking here of individual cases, for obviously there may be imaginative writers who will mature and flourish in a cozy academic environment, who will find in it material for anything they are impelled to create; we are speaking of a tendency. We need never worry about the individual genius, whether he sits in a wheat field or a seminar; but we have already noted that a culture is more than the sum of its geniuses, and we may wonder as to the prospects for a literature emerging from the universities in the next decade that will not be ingrown, precious or desiccated, that will evoke in some way the spiritual climate of two hundred million Americans far removed from the academic atmosphere.

The new writer may with justification retort that the economic situation already described makes it almost impossible for him to play, read and dream (all of which it would seem that a novelist must do, in his youth if not later) without the sheltering arm of the university, the meal ticket of the Ph.D., and the security that will alone free him to write unprofitable novels. This complaint has already been answered far better than I could by the brilliant young journalist Dan Wakefield, in an article in the June 23, 1956, number of the *Nation* entitled "Sailing to Byzantium: Yeats and the Young Mind." Replying to those members of his own generation who opt for security, crying that it is no longer possible for those now coming of age to go forth and encounter the reality of experience as it was, for example, after the First World War, Mr. Wakefield asserts: "But it has always been impossible. It was just as impossible when Hemingway lived on potatoes in Paris. The difference today is that the young are so willing to accept the impossibility."

Without attempting to dictate to my juniors, I should like to conclude my own brief consideration of this problem by noting that just as the problem is different for men of twenty and men of forty, so it assumes different aspects for single men and married men. No aspiring young writer has yet given convincing reasons why it is impossible for him to exist marginally, from one job to the next, while he learns something of the world, nor an incontrovertible statement of the absolute necessity for digging in at a university before marriage and dependents ultimately force the issue of security and stability.

Obviously, however, if young writers are obsessed with security, that obsession is a function of the society in which they live as much as their choice of theme, comparative unpopularity, consequent separation from their audiences, exploitation by publishers, and mishandling or neglect by critics more ambitious than devoted; and it can no more be wholly exorcised by exhortation than can the other ills we have been compelled to categorize.

If it were possible for the novelist to take his place as a productive and accepted member of society, most of the complaints we have been analyzing thus far would doubtless recede into their properly trivial proportions. It was not Karl Marx but Henry

James who asserted that "the future of fiction is intimately bound up with the future of the society that produces and consumes it." In a society which babbles interminable platitudes about battling for the minds and hearts of men even while it demonstrates in a thousand ways that it values the football coach and the sales engineer above the novelist and the poet, we can expect nothing but a continuation of the circumstances which drive the novelist not only into a marginal position—bad enough in itself—but into marginal utterances. So arise the false dichotomy between "affirmative" and "negative" writing and the vicious spiral of neglect, in turn isolating the writer even further and forcing him yet further to feed on himself and his similars instead of on the social body for his material. The impossible economic situation resulting from his isolation forces him into the insulated little world of the university, from which he produces work received by the critics not with interest, attention or even compassion, but with envy and malice, treated as an object of scorn and seized on as an opportunity for self-aggrandizement.

In these circumstances it would seem all the more creditable that such works as those I have mentioned by name have recently appeared, testimony to the vitality of the form and the unlikelihood of its absorption by new mass media or of its dwindling into a hobby of hyperintellectual academicians. Mr. Gore Vidal, a novelist as well as a television playwright, has expressed (in the *New York Times Book Review*) an honest fear: "After some three hundred years the novel in English has lost the general reader (or rather the general reader has lost the novel) and I propose he will not again recover his old enthusiasm."

It is Mr. Vidal's thesis that "the general reader" is now the general looker, and that "the fault, if it be a fault, is not the novelist's (I doubt if there ever have been so many interesting and excellent writers as there are now working) but the audience's," which has turned from the mediocre novel to the television play.

The mediocre novelist, says Mr. Vidal (more gracefully than my paraphrase), is already in the process of retooling for the better-paying production of television plays, leaving to the genuinely creative man the minuscule audience that has been the poet's in recent years.

Mr. Vidal's question is a fair one: Are we witnessing the decline of an individual art form concomitantly with the birth of a collective art form? Is the highbrow novel destined to join the poem as the property of a handful of intellectuals while the journeyman novelist hastens to provide the mass audience with speaking shadows for their twenty-one-inch screens?

This is somewhat different, and surely of more moment than, say, Frank O'Connor's assertion that with D. H. Lawrence "the period of the novel has gone by," since technical definitions which would exclude from the realm of the novel some of the greatest fictional achievements of the past thirty years are—however entertaining and provocative—hardly germane to the broader problems under discussion here.

Mr. Vidal bases his somewhat depressing conclusion on his interpretation of the tastes of the mass public today, as expressed in the purchase of paper books, "consuming haphazardly rather than reading." But can we not come to an opposite conclusion on the basis of a different interpretation of the same evidence? Just as it is difficult to share Mr. Vidal's optimism about the future of the television drama ("ten new 'live' plays a week: from such an awful abundance, a dramatic renaissance *must* come"—but must it? What came from the awful abundance of radio but the sonorous dramas of Norman Corwin and Arch Oboler, and an enormous increase in the power of the detergent manufacturer and the advertising agency to corrupt and debase the public taste? What has come from this new abundance thus far but a gluey, patronizing portrait of the "little guy" acclaimed as bold and courageous playwriting because it is couched in a liberalese rhetoric at once defiant and meaningless?), so it is difficult to share his pessimism about the future of the novel and of the public which consumes it in its new paperback format.

The fact is that the novelist has not lost his audience. The paperbook industry has demonstrated incontrovertibly that the public for the modern novel is from ten to twenty times as large as one would have gathered from its hard-cover sales: good novels which sell from 5,000 to 20,000 copies at $3.00 or $4.00 sell from 50,000 to 500,000 at $0.35 or $0.50. This is not simply because the reprinted novels are disguised with misleadingly vulgar covers for people who haphazardly consume rather than read, for many of them do not have such covers, and many could not compete textually with those leafed through by consumers on the prowl for titillation. Nor is it simply because they form part of an undifferentiated mass of Westerns, mysteries and science fiction, for we know now that certain paper books do not sell, and that certain others draw appreciative correspondence from readers who would never write letters about hard-cover novels—and perhaps never read them.

It would seem elementary that good modern novels sell in large quantities in paper covers to a public of hitherto unsuspected size for two perfectly good and obvious reasons: first, they are within the price range of people who want to fill their shelves but cannot afford to spend $50 a year on novels; second, they are available. The well-stocked bookshop is in all seriousness one of the glories of Western civilization—but there simply are not enough of them to fill the vast American spaces, nor are the 1,200-odd that we do have accessible to fast-moving, suburban-spreading commuter Americans.

We have already remarked that Wright Morris, as an example, goes largely unread. To my knowledge only one of his novels has as yet appeared in a cheap paper edition (in itself not as astonishing as one might expect—none of the novels of Jean Stafford have as yet been reprinted), and we have therefore no way of judging the true potential of his audience. Would we not be justified in guessing, on the basis of the comparatively astronomical paper-cover sales of writers of quality like Saul Bellow and Carson McCullers, that there are at least 50,000 Americans who would seek out the novels of Wright Morris and who would gain from them some new insight into the conditions of their lives?

Granted that the 50,000 potential readers of Wright Morris or the 250,000 actual readers of Saul Bellow are scarcely a fraction of the millions who are nourished solely by the television playwrights; granted even that a portion of these thousands are haphazard buyers who consume rather than read; nevertheless we can fairly assume the existence of a substantial fraction as regular readers of serious novels—provided that these novels are easily accessible and cheaply priced. In absolute numbers they may be small, indeed tiny in comparison with the agency-estimated millions who watch any given television play: still, they are more than the 2,000 or 3,000 who buy $4.00 novels (if they were not, both the novelist and his audience would truly be disappearing and undiscoverable in a country of 170,000,000 people).

What is more, their number is increasing. Just as America has more autos every year, more electric blankets, more people, so also it has more intellectuals. Of course, most of these are going to be mass oriented and in that mood for liberal self-congratulation already noted, but a by no means negligible number of the rising total are demonstrating their receptivity to what is new and upsetting: if the number of buyers of Van Gogh prints rises in direct ratio to the number of college graduates, so does the number of those disturbed and excited by abstract-expressionist American painters, although these latter are few in comparison with the Van Gogh discoverers; so with the new publics for the fiction of both the best-seller and the more ambitious varieties. It is the responsibility of the intelligent reader to determine which public to identify himself with and, having determined, to broaden its base among those he likes.

The more rational approach, it would seem therefore, would not be to consign the novelist and his reader to the ranks of a radical and hopelessly shrinking minority, but to begin to attempt (as Knopf, Doubleday, Ballantine and a few other publishers have already done somewhat abortively) to connect the new writer and the new reader by making the economic leap and bringing out new novels in cheap editions of 25,000 and 50,000 rather than in expensive editions of 2,500 and 5,000.

We have to consider in addition, and finally, just what it is that this rather special public expects of the novel—which raises the question of the position of the novelist in our society. One of the first critics to place this question in its contemporary context was Van Wyck Brooks, who, in an essay entitled "The Silent Generation" (in his *The Writer in America*), has opposed "curative" to "diagnostic" writers, and has pleaded with American novelists to "break the evil spell that weighs upon their minds."

Mr. Brooks asks: "Do not most contemporary tastes suggest that people read now for help in the solution of their problems, their predicaments and plights, rather than for the objective interest that readers in so-called normal times found in Shakespeare or Molière or Goethe or Dickens? . . . In short do not people nowadays read mainly for aid in the quest for security, which has become the general quest of our time in a world that has come to seem as irremediably evil as the post-Roman world of the early Middle Ages?"

I trust that by now my own attitude toward these questions has become clear, if only by implication. The best American novelists today are not invariably the least popular, but they are surely not the most popular, and the odds are that most of them cannot earn a living from their books. The most popular novelists in the

United States today, the Sloan Wilsons and the Herman Wouks, are the "curative" writers, the novelists who do in striking fashion offer "aid in the quest for security." A critic as extraordinarily erudite and sensitive as Mr. Brooks would surely not take Mr. Wouk or Mr. Wilson as his literary exemplars in preference to some of the writers I have mentioned earlier. But it is the Wouks and the Wilsons who are not even aware of a spell weighing upon their minds, who are deliberately engaged in offering their readers a "solution of their problems"; these, and the television playwrights who, as Gore Vidal implicitly concedes, are destined to be the purveyors of the second-rate.

If our best writers are "diagnostic" rather than "curative," it is not because an evil spell weighs upon their minds (at least, no more than other creative minds have always been oppressed by an evil spell), or because they deliberately choose to write for the coterie rather than for the mass audience, or because they are turning their backs on their historic function. It is rather, I am profoundly convinced, because they are paying the penalty for working in a society which has never granted the creative artist a legitimate place in its communal life.

The unfortunate truth is that the novelist in America has never been either an accepted member of a closely knit intellectual élite, as has his English counterpart, or a culture hero and intellectual leader, as has his French counterpart. There are no American novelists who speak regularly on radio and television to their fellow citizens as, for example, V. S. Pritchett does in England. There are no American novelists who write regularly on matters of national and international interest for the daily newspapers as, for example, François Mauriac and Albert Camus do in France. When Robert Penn Warren speaks his mind as a novelist and a Southerner on the question of segregation, the publication of his remarks is regarded as a special coup by *Life* magazine instead of as a logical part of the literate and intelligent intercourse on the question, and must be placed between covers before it can be soberly evaluated. When William Faulkner is invited by Dwight Eisenhower to form a committee of writers to propose ways of making the United States better liked, the invitation is not taken for granted as would be a similar request to a network executive or an advertising agency official: questions of motive inevitably arise. Even those writers who have agreed to participate in the program must wonder whether William Faulkner's name would ever have occurred to Mr. Eisenhower's advisers (that it is unthinkable that it would ever have occurred independently to the President is only another symptom of the condition I am describing) if Mr. Faulkner had not received international publicity attendant upon his acceptance of a foreign award.

There is no logical reason why American novelists should not be invited to participate in the formation of public opinion as they are in other countries; nevertheless they are not. There is no logical reason why the pronouncements of novelists on such questions as the control of international waterways, the control of atomic energy, or the control of race prejudice would be any more ridiculous than similar pronouncements by industrialists running military establishments, generals running industrial establishments, financiers running scientific establishments, and lawyer-theologians running diplomatic establishments, all of them eagerly sought after on all occasions and reproduced in all mass media; nevertheless novelists' opinions even on cultural and humanitarian matters are sought after only when a propaganda point is to be scored.

The novelist in America is not only negatively regarded as a man unfitted by background or training to contribute to the formation of intelligent attitudes on public affairs: he is positively regarded as a kind of freak unless he retreats to the university or hits the jackpot in the mass media. Inevitably what he *does* also is regarded as freakish, unless his book strikes it rich.

In a commercial culture in which the writer is held in so little esteem, in which his craft is not respected, in which there is no sense of kinship between writer and reader, we can hardly expect that his will be the loudest in the chorus of affirmative voices.

I hope that what I have said in the foregoing pages is not interpreted as either a cry of pity for the poor novelist or a plea for absolute indulgence for every piece of fiction he publishes in this country. In actuality if we view his task with eyes unclouded by ennui, venom, or anger that he is not repeating the work of the eighteenth and nineteenth century masters, we must see that he is faced in America with the most dreadful obstacles and the most challenging raw materials, the most clamorous competition and the most singular expectations, the most dangerous pitfalls and the most extraordinary potentialities. I venture to suggest that the coming decade's frenetic rate of technological development, mass-media expansion and suburban growth will make the novelist's America of the sixties more different from Scott Fitzgerald's America than Fitzgerald's America was from Edith Wharton's. Increase in difference will mean increase in difficulties, but we have no reason to fear that the artist of the future will prove any more cowardly than the artist of the past.

With every passing year there will be not less, but more people anxious to learn what he has to say. With every passing year there will be an increasing conviction that all of the answers are not necessarily to be got from the findings of groups, committees, boards and teams, or from punch cards fed into machines, or even from the efforts of men pooling their crafts and skills in the theater, the movies and television, but that awareness and understanding of doubt, complexity, anguish and triumph may still be gained as one man listens to another, as one man reads the words that another has written to him and to all his kind.

If the novelist clings to that most unselfish (in its ultimate effects) of all selfish beliefs, faith in himself, then even in a world seemingly more than ever aimless, irreligious and trapped in its own confounding contradictions, his voice will have to be heard. In the confused meantime, let him inscribe on his banner the words of the great artist whose lines inspired and hence are to be found at the beginning as well as at the close of these reflections: "The more we consider it the more we feel that the prose picture can never be at the end of its tether until it loses the sense of what it can do. It can do simply everything, and that is its strength and its life."

Jessamyn West
The Slave Cast Out

WHY DOES a writer of stories choose to write about stories instead of writing another story? The answers, I suppose, are as various as the writers who on occasion make this choice. My own answer is very simple. I do it for the same reason Arnold said he read the ancients, "in the sincere endeavor to learn and practice what is sound and true." I write about novel writing to learn about novel writing, just as the skin diver, the sprinter, the golfer draws back from doing to examine the means of execution. This may seem self-centered, selfish, egotistical. Whoever claimed the writer was anything else? I have no ax to grind, no desire to instruct, no complaints to lodge. Here I differ from Arnold who, in the Preface to his *Collected Poems* from which I have already quoted, did complain. The critics, he said, gave bad advice to writers; but this he was prepared to put up with. "It is the uncertainty," Arnold wrote, "which is dis-

194

heartening, and not the hostile criticism. How often I have felt
this when reading words of disparagement or cavil. That it is the
uncertainty as what is to be really aimed at which makes our
difficulty, not the dissatisfaction of the critic who himself suffers
from the same difficulty."

I cannot believe that Arnold would have been any happier if
the critics had, in a general meeting, come to some unanimity of
opinion as to what ailed poetry and had made recommendations
to which they all subscribed for the betterment of the next season's crop. Nor can I believe that Arnold, even after having received this unanimous critical verdict, would have relished the
unanimity or, unless it echoed Arnold, have been willing to abide
by it; and no more can I believe that, having aimed at and missed
this target, universally agreed upon, Arnold would not have been
disheartened. I must confess that I find failure disheartening—
as I would also find unanimity of opinion as to how to succeed
disheartening. It is the critics' very uncertainty which gives me
heart and hope. They assay, weigh, and condemn—but for a variety of reasons. An advent is noticed, progress and development
are commented upon, decay is prophesied. But form and subject
matter are rarely foreseen and can never be prescribed. Storytelling persists, though the nature of the story and the method of
telling change as tellers and listeners change. If critics think these
changes should come faster or should take other directions or that
storytelling itself should change, this interests me—and for two
reasons.

First of all, critics are a part of the natural (as contrasted with
the literary) world, and this is, as a writer, my subject. They are
on the scene, less vivid perhaps than ranchers or children but alive
and, as we say, kicking. Second, writing is their subject matter;
they make a profession of examining and reporting upon the pro-
ductions of writers. Now I would not attempt to define the function of the critic (to define functions is the critic's function), but

since I cannot believe that he desires either to work in a vacuum or to speak only to other critics, a part of his function must be to tell us, readers and writers, what he finds in the poems, the novels, the stories he reads. As a reader I hope by my reading of criticism to be led to greater and more discriminating enjoyment of the poem, the novel, the story. As a writer I hope this reading will forward my effort "to learn and practice what is sound and true."

So, reading critics today, I learn that the novel is played out. As a writer in the midst of writing a novel, this report naturally interests me. I feel somewhat like a typesetter reading of the invention of the linotype, or a toiler in a scriptorium seeing a page from Gutenberg. Worse! These are crafts which the hand has picked up, and what the hand has picked up the hand can pick up again. But storytelling is more than hand deep. If *it* has played out, I am going to be subjected to something more radical than technological displacement.

What does it mean, I ask myself, to say that the novel is played out? The novel is a story; and a story is causality as seen operating in the lives of human beings. Since neither human beings, causality nor the interest of human beings in either themselves or causality is played out, I'm not sure. Sometimes the critics' dissatisfaction appears to be less a reflection of the state of the novel than of their own synapses. The critic wants the old sweet shock which he feels he has recently been denied, the shock of a world presented to him in a new way. And a world presented in a new way, is, for all impractical purposes, a new world. The novelist is being asked, it sometimes appears to the novelist, to spearhead a breakthrough into a new fictional method, not because a new world exists, but because the nerve endings of certain critics have become jaded. The writer is asked to find narrative methods which will involve the critic at once more delicately and more completely in the fictional world than he finds himself involved by present methods.

196

Or, if the novelist can not touch old nerve endings more sensitively, he is asked to find new ones altogether.

Some writers, like a boy saddened by the subsiding reaction of a severed frog's leg to applications of salt, combat this falling away of critical responsiveness by laying the salt on thicker and thicker; and finally, when salt no longer turns the trick at all, resort to stronger caustics, to acids and electric shocks. But more of the same here is beating a dead horse. Though the question is, Which horse is dead? Novel? Critic? Novelist? Or all to a degree?

The reader (and this includes critics) who would not wish to experience in his own time and on his own person what readers experienced in the time of other fictional breakthroughs would be a dolt. Likewise the writer who does not wish to be the Flaubert or Proust of his day. Such wishes on the part of readers and writers are necessary if the novel is to continue to do what the greatest novels of the past have done: that is, not "mirror life" but "be" life in a way which is more significant than is life itself. But these legitimate wishes are often so voiced by the critics as to suggest that what is wanted is novelty for its own sake, "a gratification of curiosity and rhetorical sense," Arnold called it, and listed it as one of the critical demands liable to lead the writer away from the effort "to learn and practice what is sound and true." Mr. Fiedler wrote recently as if the whole duty of the novelist were, through the use of new fictional methods, to keep the Fiedler nervous system tingling. From Mr. Fiedler's point of view this is at least one of the duties of the novelist, though the novelist may be excused for taking wider views and remembering that fruitful new fictional methods were never developed for any such purposes; nor for themselves; but only for the purpose of conveying, more effectively than the old methods permitted, insights about human beings and their relations.

These insights belong often to the age, before they are bodied forth by the writer; but the bodying forth of a general insight in a specific fiction may make apparent and usable to a generation or generations what has not been usable before. For the novel, as I said, does more than reflect, is more than a mirror for the age or the ages. There is a life in it which the reader, coming to the experience openly, lives through rather than reads through; and lives through with a greater awareness of significance than he might have done at street or bedroom level. The good novel is a part of the experienced life of the good reader; it is not merely a comment upon life. It is not "about" love, for instance. It is human beings loving, and that loving so selected as to have a meaning beyond what is visible to the unselective eye peeking through the unselected keyhole.

The methods by which the life in the novel is made available to readers may change for one reason and must change for another. They *may* change for the simple pleasure a craftsman has in designing new casks for old wine; for the novelist is a craftsman and even, perhaps especially, if he has nothing new to say, he takes pleasure in hunting new ways to say it. Fictional methods *may* change for the undeniable pleasure one would have in keeping Mr. Fiedler awake. But the methods *must* change when they become inadequate for bodying forth a changed kind of human being; or a change in the novelist's or the age's understanding of human beings.

Critics, when they say the novel is played out, can be making either or both of these statements. They can be saying that the world and its inhabitants have so changed since the novels of Trollope and Dickens and Tolstoi were written that a new form is needed to deal with a new content. Or they can be saying that while people and the world are relatively unchanged they, as readers, are now so constituted as to be unable to get at the life in a novel which begins, "At the close of a wintry day in 1849 an alert observer might have seen a solitary rider picking his careful way across a snowy ridge in the Cheviot hills."

A serious novelist has no desire to struggle to give life to phantoms dwelling on an earth which has already vanished. And all novelists, serious or light, prefer, given the choice, to be read rather than unread. Nevertheless a novelist can not take the critics' word for these matters—even if the critics agree. The novelist wants readers, but before he meets the needs of readers he must satisfy his own needs, and the needs of his subject matter. Otherwise his fiction is a catered affair, no living feast, and he a panderer, and no creator. And pandering is pandering whether the client is an intellectual with exacerbated nerve endings or a simpler man emotionally satisfied with routine violence followed by a routine clinch. Differences in clients will depend largely upon what the writer can't control: his own talents and capabilities. When what a writer needs to say coincides with what a good many people want to hear, a popular book is the result. When what he needs to say coincides with what readers need to hear it may be more than popular. It may be good. The coincidence of these two needs is not very common; nor is it helped, probably, by a writer's reading of criticism.

There is no royal path to good writing; and such paths as exist do not lead through neat critical gardens, various as they are, but through the jungles of self, the world and of craft. Any serious novel is the result of a writer's struggle with himself, the world in which he lives, and the means at hand or which he develops, to body forth this world fictionally.

Writers speak of the last two, of the "times" and of "craft" more often than of the first. Civil wars are too bloody for easy progress reports. And there is also the matter of taste. A writer may, with taste unchallenged, speak of all of his troubles save his literary ones. His struggles marital, extramarital, alcoholic, financial and political may be aired over and over again for gain, for solace or for pure entertainment, and no brows will be lifted. But let him breathe one word of his struggle with a fictional love scene or even of his difficulty in writing simple declarative sentences, and readers of all kinds are going to be shocked. Such revelations appear to be more than a self-betrayal, which any reader can take and smack his lips over without flinching. The reader can accept and even relish a writer's report of his failures with women, his creditors, and his ulcers. These reports do nothing but enhance the reader's opinion of himself; he, though he can't write of life, at least knows how to live it properly. But any confession that writing itself represents a struggle hurts us as readers. Who wants to hear that the mittens Santa Claus left were the result of someone's incessant bungling efforts and were never intended, actually, to be fingerless but turned out thus only because of a lack of skill?

Just as the suicide seems to betray us all by his repudiation of the belief we all cherish, that life is worth living, so the writer who confesses that his own vision is achieved only by desperate effort undermines our faith in the authenticity of what, to enjoy, we must accept as authentic.

Other, less disinterested, motives are also involved in this literary reticence—face saving, for instance. The novelist, like any other fabricator, does not want his product judged either by the ease or by the laboriousness of fabrication. He has seen Trollope underestimated because he could put novels together during fifteen-minute waits in railway stations, and a Faulkner novel, because it was produced for purposes of shock. The product should not be judged by the process; but the minute the writer mentions process he invites this kind of judgment. A motive far deeper than any regard for taste, than any tenderness for the illusions of readers, than any concern about face saving often keeps the writer silent about his writing. This silence comes from a reverence for what he feels to be less trivial, less passing too, he hopes, than the life of his body—and that is the life of his imagination.

Nevertheless, whether confessed or not, this struggle with the self is continuous; and while the reader does well to be unconcerned with the conditions under which the novelist writes, the novelist himself, attempting to "practice what is sound and true," had better be aware of them. By "conditions" I refer to nothing trivial; not a house in the country nor times of peace, nor health nor sickness nor critical approbation or its lack. Nor am I speaking of anything as superficial as "self-expression." Who cares whether Old Ernie "expressed himself" or not when he wrote of his fisherman? Though I presume he did. It is very difficult not to express one's self; one chews, even, with a rhythm which is self-expressing. I am not speaking of anything so unimportant as what is referred to as therapy. Whether a writer loses his mind or regains it, develops an ulcer or cures it during the writing of a novel is of very little moment to us. I am speaking of what the novelist, as novelist, knows or attempts to know about himself, and I do not mean conditions of health, mental or physical; he's willing to gamble with these; I mean a condition of being far more fundamental, that state which Chekhov in a letter to a brother who wanted to write, referred to as "the slave cast out"; and which Katherine Mansfield called "purity" and Tolstoi called "holiness." For me that struggle is toward what, for lack of a better word, I call "openness" and the discovery of a true voice. The two are very closely related, since it is only through openness that the true voice can emerge.

I am not sure whether "true voice" conveys the meaning I want it to. Once when in speaking of a story I hoped to write I said, "The most difficult thing is to decide who is speaking," I was thought to have had "angle of vision" or "point of view" in mind, some matter of internal craftsmanship. Not at all. I meant that, while this story is being written, I must be able to answer the question, "Who is holding the pen?" If too many cooks spoil the broth, too many persons (and a writer is necessarily more than one person) not only spoil the story, they don't get it written.

Queasy takes out what brave puts in. Female slows down what male accelerates. Intellectual muddies what instinctive clarifies. The result of this embarrassment of persons brings the pen to a standstill and the story to a hodgepodge.

Sometimes it is only by writing the story that the novelist can discover—not his story—but its writer, the official scribe, so to speak, for that narrative. V. S. Pritchett answered the question, "Why do you write?" by saying, "To find out who I am." Writing is a way of playing parts, of trying on masks, of assuming roles, not for fun but out of desperate need, not for the self's sake but for the writing's sake. "To make any work of art," says Elizabeth Sewell, "is to make, or rather to unmake and remake one's self."

Now, while the "true voice" represents a selection, a discovery, a constellation, the paradox is that it can be discovered, selected, constellated only through openness; and that only openness permits the true voice, once discovered, to flow, to soar. By openness I do not mean "open-mindedness" nor "openness to experience"; though these states might well attend the kind of openness of which I speak. Perhaps I had better say what this openness is not. It is not self-protection. It is not hatred. It is not impatience. It is not answers. It is not facts. It is not justification. It is not pride. It is not a fist, it is not a clenching.

It is exposure. It is space. Without space, without openness, the world of the novel cannot grow. It can only be made. "Growth," you may say, "can take place in a very small space. A seed may sprout and grow in a space as narrow as a hair, while to make a table of any size several square feet are needed." This is to forget not only the nature of growth but vertical dimensions. A taproot can travel to China, and a crown forest need not, if its nature requires it, stop short of the stars. These are the dimensions of growth. A clenching kills. And hate, which is a clenching, which is a focusing of great narrowness, kills. There is not room for growth inside what, to be useful as a weapon, must exclude space and become solid matter. Hate can produce writing as explosive as a blow; but it is utilitarian writing, words put together not to reveal but to destroy. There may be no life in this writing, but we are interested in the life behind the writing. It is that to which we respond.

Openness, persisted in, destroys hate. The novelist may begin his writing with every intention of destroying what he hates. Since a novelist writes of persons this means the destruction (through revelation) of an evil person. But writing in openness, which means a becoming and not a describing or talking about, the writer becomes the evil person, does what the evil person does, for his reasons and with his justifications. As this takes place, as the novelist opens himself to evil, a self-righteous hatred of evil is no longer possible. The evil which now exists is within; and one is self-righteous in relation to others, not to one's self. Just as the man who pities is suspect unless he himself has experienced the pitiable state, or is willing to enter it if that will help, so is the novelist suspect who writes of evil without openness to evil. Evil, bodied forth in fiction, is the writer himself assuming the aspects of evil. Now that he has himself assumed the aspects of evil and does not condemn from the outside magisterially, he can bring to his readers understanding and elicit from them compassion. This is why we do not, as readers, hate the great villains of literature. Milton does not hate Satan, nor Thackeray, Becky; nor Shakespeare, Macbeth. For a time Milton was Satan; Thackeray, Becky; Shakespeare, Macbeth. And the openness of the novelist (together with his talent and his skill) permits us, his readers, though we know that Satan must be cast down and that Macbeth must die, to respond to them without narrowness, with understanding, and hence with compassion instead of hatred.

We do not love them, however; nor do I think this "openness" of which I have been speaking can be called love, though it must include the possibility of love as it includes the possibility of evil. Perhaps what I call openness is what Keats calls "negative capability." But by whatever name we call it, the struggle with the self is an effort, in large part, to maintain this state. Without openness the personal, the true voice can not be found; without openness the writing must remain superficial and narrow. The writing may of course remain so anyway. Openness will not supply talent or craft or industry or intelligence or relatedness of enough significance to other human beings to give the writer understanding of himself or others. But openness permits these to exist and develop.

If the writing of any serious novel represents the writer's struggle with himself, the world and his craft, his struggle with the world is most bitter, vital and meaningful as it relates to this necessary state of openness. Whatever in the world obstructs or prevents it is the enemy of writers and of literature. I doubt if, in this respect, the world for writers has changed much.

Many writers, Arnold being neither the first nor the last, have found their own times inhospitable. Arnold, who deplored the critics' lack of agreement, was not pleased by their occasional agreements, either. They valued, he said, "the language above the action, not the action itself." "False, absolutely false aims" are prescribed by the critics in asking, as they did, for "a true allegory of the state of one's own mind in a representative history." This true allegory is still being asked for, a request which Frank O'Connor, a less unlikely companion for Arnold than one might think, has in his recent *The Mirror in the Roadway* repudiated as vigorously as Arnold. "When I want to know what Ireland is thinking I look in my own heart," O'Connor quotes Joyce, and remarks, "This is symbolist doctrine with a vengeance." Both Arnold and O'Connor believe that a desire to learn what Ireland is thinking might be better satisfied by looking at what Ireland is thinking. And with critics today urging "true allegories," writing tends to become either-or: either the look at Ireland or the look at "my own heart." Openness might permit the entrance of both into the novel.

Evil and its specific manifestation in sin had a meaning, in past times, which if it served no other purpose was dramatically useful to the novelist. Sin has now been replaced by violence and does not develop in the novel, no matter what its horsepower of raw energy outside the novel, the functional torque of one small relevant sinful act. The novel, without this torque, does not engage itself efficiently with the reader.

The unique person, the individual whom the writer used to address, write about and try to be, has had his uniqueness diluted and his edges blurred. His mind is today fed on slogans, his body on synthetics. He lives and dies en masse and values himself for his ability to do so. "I am not asking for anything anyone else can't have," he says, with the modern sin of pride in having none; and forgetting that no one can "have" what he can't use, he thus feeds smugness upon conformity. How is a man who has failed socially or institutionally (do we recognize any other kind of failure today?) described? We say he, "got out of line." Whatever *for?* What a man has to get out of line to do is today suspect. Perhaps the novelist must recognize that evil changes its aspects from age to age and that praise of the mask blinds us to what the mask covers; perhaps part of our struggle with the world is the struggle to recognize the new masks which evil puts on.

The reader also is a part of the world, and in so far as he values the shoddy, the trivial, the false, the novelist must oppose him also. The reader's love of the "true story" is no help to the novelist. The wars produced more violence and cruelty, courage and devotion than the novelists of the world can equal, statistically, working from now till doomsday. These firsthand accounts satisfy the reader's hankering for facts and convince him that reality is what happened at a named place on a specific day. And the novels he reads in quantity tend to be either nostalgic turnings away from the "facts" or the "facts" made even more irresistible by being attached to a narrative hook of that romantic-sexual nature for which frail human flesh seems to have been made.

These are but a few of the complaints made about the "world" when the writer speaks of his "struggle with the world." I want to mention them only in passing to show that I know they exist. The world of which I speak and against which the writer must struggle is not this exterior world which he recognizes and with which, because he does recognize it, he *can* struggle, but the world which has become so much a part of him that he accepts it as himself. This world, bred into his bone by his times, his up-bringing and his education, and of which more often than not he is unaware, the writer must repudiate if he is, through openness, to find his own voice.

Now we are back once again with Chekhov and his exhortation to "cast the slave out." "The slave cast out" is the real title of every great novel; which is to say of every novel which has thrown off the shackles of the apparent and the temporal. Writers have had many names for the shackles from which they knew they must free themselves before they could write truly. But however named, they include the attributes which result from being narrowly brought up, taught envy and suspicion and pride and intolerance from the cradle; from being persuaded that the supreme achievements are to be as "independent as a hog on ice"; to own property and to owe no man money; to confide in no one and to accept no confidences; to give, but never to take, since taking imposes obligations; to claim nothing, protest nothing, expect nothing, but to get everything; to compete, but to keep the fact quiet; to win, but not celebrate (if the neighbors don't find it out there *is* no failure); to shrink from the new, the outspoken, the spontaneous; to ignore the self as body, the mind as creator, the human being as artist (and vice versa), the world as a source of art and God as love. This is the world ingrained, the world as self and the self as slave. Freedom from this enslavement requires that one unmake and remake oneself. To do so is to die on the chance, and without any promise, of resurrection. The artist, as such, has no savior. He must unmake before he can start to remake, and without any assurance that remaking is possible. One must unmake, remain open without any conviction that the chief, perhaps the only, entrant won't be pain. This is what I mean by the writer's "struggle with the world"—not a struggle with the times, with its taste for facts rather than truths, with good faith replaced by bad faith, belief by realism, sin by violence, uniqueness by conventionality. These are no help to a novelist, but before he can cope with them he *must* cope with what is ingrained; to see the world, he must not *be* the world. Insight, not self-sight, is needed.

This is perhaps the place to speak of craft, for in speaking of the world I have already spoken of subject matter, and the choice of subject matter is a part of craft. The novelist, endeavoring "to learn and practice what is sound and true" (myself, I permit myself to believe on optimistic mornings), has now got himself into a favorable position, at least, for writing. Open, with a true voice, the slave cast out, nothing now remains except the prodigious work of writing his novel: that is, of creating a world with words. Looked at in the most elementary way, the novel involves two elements: a subject and a manner of presenting that subject. And in the best novels these two so fuse that there is no adequate way of reporting the happening except in the author's words. And one needs not only the words of the single episode one is attempting to paraphrase, but the words which have preceded it and those which will follow. For the whole of the good novel clings together, adheres like the notes of a melody, each note more in context, because of memory of what came before and anticipation of what is to follow. Nevertheless the two can be separated, and when we do so we find that critics today object less to the stories novels tell than the way in which these stories are told. The critic's nerves, so sensitive to manner, are hardier when it comes to content; "if we are to move forward . . ." (in novel writing, Mr. Fiedler means) "analysis must be replaced by projection." What novelists are to stop analyzing and what they are to begin projecting is not specified. This is perhaps unimportant enough to be left to the novelist himself.

In this the modern critic is unlike Arnold, though he resembles the critics Arnold was criticizing; the men who did not say to the writer, "All depends upon subject; choose a fitting action, penetrate yourself with the feelings of its situations; this done everything else will follow," as Arnold believed they should have done.

Before questioning whether or not everything else will really follow, including "projection" instead of "analysis," we need to know what Arnold considers a "fitting action." A fitting action is one, he says, which "most powerfully appeals to the great primary human affections; to the elementary part of our nature, to our passions; that which is great and passionate is eternally interesting; and interesting solely in proportion to its greatness and its passion." For these reasons Arnold finds the action of *The Excursion* and *Hermann and Dorothea* less excellent than that of the *Iliad* or the episode of Dido. In these latter cases "the action is greater, the personages nobler, the situations more intense."

Arnold does admit, almost parenthetically, that these actions "should be communicated in an interesting manner," and that "construction" is involved. He is at pains to deny, however, that manner or construction comes first; and he values Shakespeare himself not for his "gift of expression" but for "his skill in dis-

208

cerning and firmly conceiving an excellent action, his power of intensely feeling a situation, of intimately associating himself with a character." Critics, if Arnold's report is accurate, have not changed greatly. The question is, have novelists? And is the current discontent with the novel less a reflection upon it as played-out form than as ill-chosen content? Do we, as novelists, refuse to imagine greatly? Are we, as we have been accused, so incapable of loving that we can no longer body forth men and women of heroic stature? Have we become so unrelated to other human beings that the novel (which is about, as Iris Murdoch says, "people's treatment of each other and so . . . about human values") is no longer possible for us?

These are all questions about subject matter, about content, about "a fitting action." I have taught at several writers' conferences and I do not remember that I or anyone else (I did not, of course, hear everyone else) spoke about "a fitting action," or an action which because it was "great and passionate" formed a suitable subject for the novel. Our concern there, as before our typewriters and writing boards, was primarily about manner, form, expression. Such an attitude has in it a kind of touching if foolish humility. We valued ourselves by the standards of academicians for what was least ourselves, for knowledge instead of understanding, arrangement instead of insight, craft instead of penetration.

It is perhaps impossible to say why novels are written. Some conclusions may be drawn however from a reading of novels. The novel says that certain people had certain experiences. But it is apparent in serious novels that their writers believe that these experiences make some comment upon life itself; that they are not without significance or relevance to us as testimonies concerning human values. And that as such, analysis or projection is but a means by which the novelist attempts to make his insights vivid, moving and convincing to his readers. If, as the existentialists say, "Existence is prior to essence," the novelist is a man who wants to eliminate as much of that priority as possible. He accepts this statement and, as a matter of fact, was a phenomenologist before the word was invented, but he is selective; by the existence which he portrays he desires to reveal essences; otherwise he is no more than a tape recorder with viscera—which means an inefficient tape recorder.

The ways of telling a story, word by word, sentence by sentence, episode by episode, through interior dialogue, no dialogue, all dialogue, from the viewpoint of a single character or with the omniscience of God, with four-letter words or twenty-letter words, with time moving forward, backward or sideways, with symbols which refer to something else or acts which are self-contained, by methods realistic, naturalistic, romantic, surrealistic, existentialist, analytic or projected, are various; but all are selected in this hope: the consuming hope that through fictional existence the reader (and the writer) may come to non-fictional meaning; may come eagerly, and rest finally in that aesthetic contentment which is the result of having experienced a manner perfectly suited to its matter.

To provide this content is not easy; nor is it made easier by the fact that the reader himself changes. He is a better reader today than he was a hundred years ago (in spite of Flesch and TV). He is capable of inferring what the older reader wanted to be told. He responds to a language much more alert, nervous and evocative. He is less awed by writing than he was and does not accept the neatness of unreal plotting simply because it is spread out in print and insisted upon through 350 pages. He has more knowledge of existence and more need of essence. Writing a novel is in many ways easier than it has ever been before, as the great number of present-day novelists proves. Writing a good novel has never been harder. So many good novels have already been written—and it is not the reader's knowledge of these masterpieces of the past which makes novel writing more difficult today, but the novelist's own knowledge. Grandma Moses can paint something which charms us because she does not have in her eyes and hands the knowledge of past greatness. She is a true primitive, is working at the top of her bent and hence delights us as a child delights us who can only stammer words but stammers them as best he can. But there can be no primitives (with rare exceptions) in the field of writing. We cannot write novels as Grandma Moses paints—as freshly as if Richardson and Fielding, Defoe and Smollett had never covered their pages. Nor can we imitate, write a *Madame Bovary* for the suburbs or be the Proust of the southern California hills. With the knowledge of what the novel has been, with the *burden* of that knowledge we must find our own and our time's means for making our personal understandings live in the novel. That is our struggle with technique. My own feeling is that it will be won and that the future of the novel depends less upon this than upon the writer's struggle with self and the world. Which is to say, I suppose, that I believe that "who" writes the novel is of more importance than how the novel is written. When we find geniuses we shall not need to dictate form. The proper, the fitting writer will find the proper manner. Such a conclusion is suitable for a novelist, since his focus must always be upon the human being; all his non-fictional abstractions tend to become the outline of a story, in this case the story of a writer trying to learn and practice what is sound and true.

Granville Hicks

Afterword: The Enemies
of the Novel

SUCH A PHRASE as "enemies of the novel" may seem hyperbole if not, indeed, evidence of paranoia, but the novel does have enemies, and it is possible to show why. The novel has had its own history, and the course of its development has been such that, as I have said in the Foreword, there are more serious novelists at work in America at the present time than there have ever been in the past. This development, however, has taken place in the midst of other developments—in the midst, in fact, of a technological revolution whose complexity we cannot even begin to comprehend. As a result not so much of technological change itself as of the uncertainties and tensions it has created, serious novelists—serious artists of every kind—are working in a culture that is largely unsympathetic to them.

The novel has always had enemies, but they have not always been the same enemies. Its earliest enemies condemned the novel as a frivolous waste of time. In his introduction to *The Scarlet Letter*, Nathaniel Hawthorne imagined one of his ancestors murmuring to the others: "What is he? A writer of story-books! What kind of business in life,—what mode of glorifying God, or being serviceable to mankind in his day and generation,—may that be? Why, the degenerate fellow might as well have been a fiddler." Scorn for the triviality of the novel persisted among many American people throughout the nineteenth century. And it still persists in some quarters: not long ago an advertisement for the *Reporter* boasted that the readers of that magazine, among many other virtues, "prefer non-fiction over fiction by a 10-to-1 vote." Of course, most novels published in the nineteenth century were, and most novels published today are, a waste of time, but now no moderately well informed person damns the novel on that account. Those who insist that the novel is dead are most emphatic in proclaiming the greatness of novels written in the good days before the fatal seizure. The talk about the death of the novel is, if one chooses to look at it that way, proof that at last the novel is taken seriously.

Then there were those, and very powerful they were less than fifty years ago, who were determined that novels should conform to their standards of morality. The freedom that the novelist enjoys today—almost no taboo topics, almost no forbidden words—was unthinkable before 1900 and only thinkable in 1920. Thanks to Theodore Dreiser, Upton Sinclair, H. L. Mencken, and a multitude of others, today's novelists do not have to worry about Anthony Comstock and his New York Society for the Suppression of Vice nor about the Watch and Ward Society of Boston. Whether they avail themselves of specific freedoms or not, novelists gain by virtue of the relief from pressure. We are reminded of what that pressure meant by a passage that Thomas Hardy entered in his journal while *Tess* was under attack: "If this sort of thing continues no more novel-writing for me. A man must be a fool to deliberately stand up to be shot at." And his next novel was his last.

The serious novelist is grateful for the routing of these enemies, but he is even more grateful for the literary achievements of his predecessors, and he understands very well how much he owes to the past. He may be a long way from being a Jamesian, but you will find that he has done his homework in James's novels—and in the prefaces, too. He knows the novelists who are currently fashionable, can tell you exactly what he thinks about Dostoievski, Melville, Kafka, and Fitzgerald, but he also has ideas about Hardy and Meredith and very possibly about Disraeli and Peacock, and he may turn out to have a respectful interest in William Dean Howells. This sort of literary awareness proves too much of a burden for some young hopefuls, but it rarely injures a writer of promise. In spite of a persistent legend, the major novelists have never been ignoramuses. Our novelists today may be more self-conscious about what they know, but serious novelists have always managed to acquaint themselves with what could be of use to them.

It is because of what the past has accomplished that we have so many serious novelists. We see nothing strange in the fact that nowadays dozens of young men and women deliberately choose the writing of novels as their vocation, train themselves strenuously for the task—today, often enough, under academic auspices—and, given the least encouragement, devote their lives to it. Yet the novel at the outset was commonly the work of amateurs. Both Richardson and Fielding came to the novel by accident. Scott turned to the novel at the age of forty-three because he was no longer successful in the writing of romantic narrative poems. Thackeray was a writer long before he was a novelist, and so was Mark Twain. A large proportion of the great novels of the nineteenth century were written by men and women who, at least in the beginning, were novelists by chance rather than by choice. At the end of the century Joseph Conrad was insisting that he would never have written another word if Edward Garnett, after reading *Almayer's Folly*, had urged him to become a novelist instead of merely suggesting that he write another novel.

The tradition that makes our serious novelists professionals is just what convinces some observers that the novel is moribund. Malcolm Cowley—no enemy of the novel!—has suggested that certain limits have been reached by such writers as Joyce, Hemingway, Faulkner, Kafka, and Mann, and that now there is nowhere for the novel to go. But how easy it would have been to say at almost any point in the history of the novel that it had reached its limits! In 1900, for instance, a critic might have surmised that Dickens and Flaubert and Zola and James and Dostoievski and Tolstoi and their contemporaries had done everything there was to be done, but then along came the five writers Mr. Cowley has named and some other limit-busters as well. The truth is that the limits of the novel are established by novelists, not legislated by critics. They are the frontiers that have been reached at any given moment, and they remain frontiers only until somebody crosses them.

But, some melancholy authority is bound to remark, nobody seems to be crossing any frontiers right now. Even if this is true— I am not at all sure that it is; we are not always conscious of such crossings at the moment they occur—despair seems premature. Geniuses are rare, and it is unreasonable to expect that they will come charging forth, one hard upon the heels of another. The health of the novel depends on the existence of such serious practitioners as we have in unprecedented abundance. The geniuses, when they come, will take care of themselves, and will take care of the limits of the novel, too.

It is apparent that all is not well with the novel today, but the problem is essentially a problem of readers, not a problem of writers. One consequence of the technological revolution is the emergence of what Donald Tovey called the Age of Inattention. I do not know how to begin to describe the distractions to which our culture subjects us. Technology has freed most of us in America from the age-old fear of going hungry, but our consumption of peace pills—those we purchase in the drugstores and those we purchase in the bookstores—suggests how many worries we have acquired. Technology has given us a great new leisure, and has devised ways of filling that leisure to overflowing. Technology has opened the whole world to us, and has laid the problems of every part of it on our doorstep. Inattention becomes indispensable to survival. Like the housewife who keeps the radio on all day, we have to learn to hear only what we want to hear. But the danger is that we shall lose, or perhaps never acquire, the ability to pay attention to anything, to listen fully, with all our being.

Fewer and fewer individuals are both able and willing to pay attention to any work of art, and this is happening at a time when the serious novel is demanding more and more effort on the part of its readers. The great novels, of course, have always rewarded effort, but in the past some of the greatest did not demand it. They could, that is, be read as stories, even though there were other and better ways of reading them. But now we have gone beyond the point of innocent compromise. The novel has been shaped in our age by writers—Joyce, Proust, Mann, Faulkner— who demanded nothing less of their readers than full attention, and to write as if these men had not existed is a betrayal of the craft, and suicide as well. The serious novel today may, like many of the great novels of the past, have elements that make it popular, but to the novelist these elements are incidental. His aim is to involve the reader in an imaginative effort, and he will settle for nothing less.

The cleavage between the popular novel and the serious novel constantly increases. The rewards of popularity, what with the book clubs, Hollywood, and TV, are now tremendous, and the commercial novelist uses all his wiles to lay hands on them. He is at home in our Age of Inattention, for he asks nothing of his readers but makes it his business to know what they want and to give it to them. The serious novelist, rejecting this venality, may be tempted to cultivate difficulty for its own sake. This happens, but less frequently than the casual reader may suppose; the novel that seems arbitrarily difficult at first reading, as *Ulysses* seemed, as *The Sound and the Fury* seemed, usually turns out to justify all the demands it makes. In general, the serious novelist is simply writing as he has to write. He can only say, with Mark Harris, "I write. Let the reader learn to read."

Perhaps a not outrageously paradoxical way of stating our dilemma would be to say that too many good novels are being written—too many, that is, in proportion to the number of people who are able and willing to read them. The enemies of the novel, in that case, might be thought of as persons who propose to solve the problem by plowing the novel under. It should be clear by now that I do not see the novel as the victim of a conspiracy on the part of a few individuals; the predicament of the novel rises out of a complex cultural situation. But the enemies, if they are not important, are symptomatic.

The middlebrow enemies of the novel simply want the serious novel to stop being serious while continuing to seem serious. One segment of middlebrow opinion, which finds expression in the Luce publications, has concrete ideas about the kind of pseudo-seriousness it is looking for: it wants our novelists to be very serious about what a fine country this is and what noble fellows businessmen are. Another, more sophisticated segment insists on seeing what it would like to believe is its own image. (How often *New Yorker* reviewers damn a novel because its characters are dull or otherwise unattractive.) In between are the spokesmen for the people who want to eat their cake and have it too, who are smart enough to recognize the shoddiness of the blatantly commercial novel but too indolent or too distracted to come to terms with the genuinely serious novel.

The middlebrows are enemies of the novel by inadvertence, so to speak; they would say that they oppose only one kind of novel, honestly unaware that this is the only kind that counts. Among the highbrows, on the other hand, we have outspoken or ill-concealed hostility. Many of the people who write about literature in the highbrow quarterlies operate under a banner on which is proudly inscribed, "I do not read modern novels," a statement to be interpreted, "Modern novels are not worth reading." There is, of course, no law requiring a critic to read contemporary literature of any kind. When Edmund Wilson writes, "I make no attempt to keep up with the younger American writers," one can only grant that he has earned the right to choose, while regretting that talents once so fruitfully devoted to contemporary literature are no longer exercised in a field that badly needs them. What one feels in many of the highbrows, however, is plain belligerence, and this can be found not only in those who ignore modern novels but also in many who read them and write about them. The fiction chronicles in the quarterlies display this belligerence much of the time. In reading such chronicles, one can detect a good deal of old-fashioned showing off, occasionally mixed with some degree of genuine discrimination, but the dominant note increasingly seems to be impatience if not anger.

Perhaps we can understand this if we recognize that the highbrows are distracted too. Not so long ago, literature courses in most colleges dealt only with people who were safely dead, and Ph.D. theses were devoted to those who had been dead a long time.

Now contemporary literature is academically respectable, so respectable that in a single university seven masters' theses were this year being written on William Faulkner. (The new importance of modern literature reflects changes in educational theory and practice that in turn reflect the impact of technological development on our society.) But the academic mind remains the academic mind—not all teachers of literature, happily, have academic minds—and it deals by preference with what can be cataloged and disposed of once for all, with what, in short, is dead. (How else can we explain the indecent eagerness of certain highbrow critics to proclaim that Hemingway and Faulkner are "finished"?) The living novel becomes for such persons an intolerable distraction. They have a stake in modern literature; they have taken it over; it is, as they will tell you, their field. How can they admit that it is in constant process of flux?

I presume that the highbrow enemies of the novel have a certain influence, if only because they provide an excuse for people who have their own reasons for ignoring modern fiction, but I do not blame them for the predicament of the novel. They merely have to be taken into account when that predicament is defined. The great majority of our fellow citizens, demanding effortless entertainment, have no interest in serious fiction, and the mass media almost guarantee that they will never by any remote chance be led to take an interest in it. An influential section of the intelligentsia is alienated, by way of its vested interests, from all contemporary creative effort. And in between, the middlebrows, already distracted by the complexities of the modern world, are further distracted and confused by the demands that some of their spokesmen make upon the novel.

The rise of the mass media, I believe, is responsible only in minor ways for the predicament of the serious novel. Technology made possible the leisure that caused the demand for mass culture, and it brought into existence the media that satisfied the demand.

Mass culture is not hostile to what is called, for want of a better term, high culture, but merely indifferent. It has by-products of great value, but its principal product is and, as far as I can see, always will be effortless entertainment. Serious fiction—genuinely imaginative work of any kind—has always been fostered by a small minority, and the situation is not altered one way or the other by the millions of hours devoted daily to the mass media. Certainly we have no reason to fear, as observers from De Tocqueville to Ortega y Gasset have feared, that mass culture will destroy high culture—except, perhaps, under totalitarian governments. We need only look around us to see that in our country, with mass culture in full bloom, the creative will is still strong. Moreover, there is reason to doubt whether mass culture, being itself uncreative, could survive indefinitely without some reservoir of creativity to draw on. The achievements of high culture become the clichés of mass culture, but if clichés didn't change once in a while, one could expect nothing but universal boredom.

We can serve the cause of serious fiction, not by attacking the mass media but by seeking ways of enlarging the small minority —that is, by trying to transform potential readers into actual readers. That there are these potential readers I have no doubt, for I encounter them all the time. It becomes clear that they can read because of the way they talk about what they have read in the past, but at a certain point I begin to draw blanks. And the proffered explanation is, "I just don't seem to get time to read novels any more," or, "I never seem to know what novels are worth reading."

Since it is one of the characteristics of the new leisure that most people, and especially people with intelligence and some sense of responsibility, have nowhere near enough time to do all the things they think they ought to do, it is hard to argue with anyone who says he hasn't time to read novels. You can't convince a conscientious doctor that he ought to read fiction instead of using his free hours to catch up with the medical journals, and you can't convince a housewife with a civic spirit that she should give up the PTA and the League of Women Voters. On the other hand, one sometimes knows and often suspects that lack of time is not the real reason. Time could be found if it were not for some feeling that the novel is one of the things one doesn't have to find time for.

More time might be found if people had a clearer idea of what novels are worth reading. I have often been asked whether there is any periodical from which a busy person can learn with reasonable accuracy what books, and especially what novels, he ought to read. The answer obviously has to be No. By reading half a dozen periodicals long enough to become familiar with the virtues and shortcomings of their reviewers, one can arrive at fairly dependable judgments, but of course nobody is going to do that who doesn't somehow or other make books his business. The average reader has to trust to luck.

The low state of literary journalism is a result of the kind of confusion I have been talking about and also one of its causes. These are the facts: 1. There are only a few dozen periodicals in the whole country in which it is conceivable that a serious novel might be given a competent review. 2. Most of these periodicals have space to review only a few books, and most of them emphasize non-fiction at the expense of fiction. 3. The two or three large book-review media are obliged to devote much of their space to popular novels, both because these are the novels in which the majority of their readers are interested and because they are the mainstay of the publishing business. As a consequence of this situation, a novel of some distinction may not receive a single review by a person who has taken the trouble to read the book.

And even if a book is reviewed, it may not be reviewed intelligently. There are not only prejudices, middlebrow and highbrow, to be taken into account; there is also incompetence. This is found not only in much run-of-the-mill daily and weekly book reviewing, done under a kind of pressure that makes the competence we sometimes encounter a miracle, but also in what one would expect to be the carefully meditated fiction chronicles in the quarterlies. What are we to make of a reviewer (in *Partisan Review*) who admits in the course of damning *The Field of Vision* that he has read nothing else by Wright Morris, and who also attempts to evaluate C. P. Snow's *Homecoming* without having read any of the other novels in the series of which it is part, a series he preposterously characterizes as a *Bildungsroman?* One is almost forced to conclude that the editors of *Partisan* regard ignorance as a major qualification for reviewers of fiction.

It is easy to understand why literary journalism happens to be in this unhappy state: there are the shrinking of the media, the uneasiness of the publishing industry in the face of inflation and new kinds of competition, the confusion of the middlebrows, and the hostility of the highbrows. But I do not know that we have to accept the situation. Here is the point at which anyone who is concerned about the contemporary novel may be able to have an influence. All any of us has to do is to find a pulpit from which he can preach, and that is not too difficult.

We shall preach, of course, to the people who can read serious fiction but don't. There are arguments, I think, to which they may listen. There is, for instance, the question of conformity in our society, a question that troubles most thoughtful persons. We can point out that the act of choosing to be a serious novelist is in itself today an act of dissent, and that the cultivation of the craft is a constant discipline in nonconformity. The novelist is always learning to communicate what he sees, and this means that he is always learning to see, to see, that is, for himself. All our days we are being fed, often forcibly fed, the mush of group opinion, until many of us long to get our teeth into the honest-to-God thoughts and feelings of a single, specific person. That is what we do when we read a serious novel. We may think that a particular novelist is cockeyed, but at least we get to know what an individual pair of eyes, defective or not, is seeing.

The novelist is not only a misfit in an Age of Conformity; he is an anomaly in an Age of Inattention. For the novelist, the paying of attention is a tool, a technique, a *raison d'être*. He is as much exposed to distractions as anyone else, but an unceasing struggle against them is the condition of success in his chosen vocation. A serious novel is by definition the work of a man who has learned to pay attention to what goes on in him and about him. And it not only brings to you and involves you in some small segment of the world that has been really looked at; it also, in a mysterious fashion, increases your own capacity for experience. The more completely you yield yourself to a novel—or any other work of art—as an experience, the less likely it is that your own experiences will be wasted on you.

The serious novel is also an act of evaluation, one performed according to a set of difficult but indispensable rules. The novelist can never allow himself to present only one side of a case; the other side must always be given. He does not make judgments, but he forces the reader to make them. As Lionel Trilling puts it, he involves the reader in the moral life. In the confusions of our society, with the onrush of new experiences and new problems, we need more than ever a talent for self-scrutiny, and the serious novel gives us practice.

The serious novel is needed, and, happily for us, it is being written. If the times are in so many ways unfavorable for the serious novelist, he is still a beneficiary of the national prosperity. He may make next to nothing from his novels, but jobs can be found, and fellowships, if not exactly abundant, are more numerous than ever before. I believe that most of our serious novelists would go hungry if they had to rather than stop writing, but few of them are compelled to make that choice. And every year, it seems, more and more young people deliberately elect this financially unrewarding way of life. We can be sure that many of them have talent, and perhaps one of them is the genius who will rout the enemies of the novel once for all.

Whether a genius appears or not, I view the future of the novel without alarm: it is safe in the hands of the men and women who have contributed to this volume and in the hands of others as talented and as devoted as they. The conditions that are largely responsible for the present neglect of the serious novel—the confusion of our society, the multitudinous distractions, the almost universal apprehensiveness—are conditions that make the operation of the imagination almost, if not quite, a matter of life and death. And the imagination is functioning in the novel, though of course not only there. Not fewer people but more are likely to become convinced that, whatever else may be expendable in contemporary American life, the serious novel isn't.

Notes on the Contributors

SAUL BELLOW was born in Canada in 1915, not long after his parents migrated to that country from Russia, but, the family having moved to Chicago in 1924, he considers himself "a Chicagoan, out and out." After spending two years at the University of Chicago, he transferred to Northwestern University, from which he was graduated in 1937 with honors in anthropology and sociology. Although he began graduate study at the University of Wisconsin, he soon turned to writing, and he published his first novel, *Dangling Man*, in 1944. He has taught at various intervals at the University of Minnesota, Princeton, New York University, Bard College, and the New School for Social Research. He has held a Guggenheim Fellowship and a National Institute of Arts and Letters Award, and *The Adventures of Augie March* won the National Book Award in fiction for 1953.

BOOKS: *Dangling Man*, 1944; *The Victim*, 1947; *The Adventures of Augie March*, 1953; *Seize the Day*, 1956.

225

PAUL DARCY BOLES was born in Indiana, and a large part of his boyhood was spent in the Midwest. He left high school without graduating, and worked in the Gary, Indiana, steel mills for three years, after which he served in the United States Army, then had jobs in Denver, Colorado, Grand Rapids, Michigan, Muskegon, Michigan, Mobile, Alabama, and Atlanta, Georgia. He has been a newspaper reporter, industrial motion picture director-producer, and TV writer-director for an advertising agency. He lives in Atlanta, where he has taught several courses in the novel at Georgia State College. His fifth novel, as yet untitled, is scheduled for publication in 1958, and he is currently working on the sixth.

BOOKS: *The Streak*, 1953; *The Beggars in the Sun*, 1954; *Glenport, Illinois*, 1956; *Deadline*, 1957.

JOHN BROOKS was born in New York City in 1920 and brought up in Trenton, New Jersey. He attended the Kent School, and was graduated from Princeton in 1942. After spending three years in the Army Air Force, chiefly in the European theater, he became a contributing editor of *Time*. Since 1949 he has been a regular contributor to the *New Yorker*, mostly to "The Talk of the Town" and "A Reporter at Large." His first novel, *The Big Wheel*, was written in part on a Eugene Saxton Memorial Fellowship. He has contributed book reviews to the *New York Times* and to *Harper's*, and in 1955 he served as a member of the National Book Award fiction jury. His third novel, *The Man Who Broke Things*, is to be published early in 1958.

BOOKS: *The Big Wheel*, 1949; *A Pride of Lions*, 1954.

RALPH ELLISON, born in Oklahoma in 1914, attended Tuskegee Institute from 1933 to 1936, with the aid of a scholarship from the State of Oklahoma. In 1936 he went to New York City to study sculpture and music composition, but soon turned to writing, and has contributed to such magazines as *Horizon*, the *Reporter*, and the *Saturday Review of Literature*. His first and so far his only novel, *Invisible Man*, was published in 1952 and was given the National Book Award in fiction for that year. In 1955 he was awarded the Prix de Rome of the American Academy of Arts and Letters, and has recently been living in Italy.

BOOK: *Invisible Man*, 1952.

HERBERT GOLD was born in Cleveland, Ohio, in 1924, and grew up in that city. During the war he served in Army Military Intelligence, and after the war took his bachelor's and master's degrees in philosophy at Columbia. In 1949-1950 he held a Fulbright Fellowship for study in France, and in 1953-1954 he had a Buenos Aires Convention grant to live and write in Haiti. He has taught at Western Reserve University, Wayne University, and the State University of Iowa. He was awarded a *Hudson Review* Fellowship in fiction in 1956, and a Guggenheim Fellowship in 1957. He has published short stories and articles in such magazines as *Atlantic Monthly*, *Hudson Review*, the *New Yorker*, *Partisan Review*, *Yale Review*, and *Commentary*. A story of his received second prize in the O. Henry Memorial Award for 1956. Several of his short stories will appear shortly in *15x3*.

BOOKS: *Birth of a Hero*, 1951; *The Prospect Before Us*, 1954; *The Man Who Was Not With It*, 1956.

MARK HARRIS, who was born in Mount Vernon, New York, in 1922, has attended Clemson College, University of New Mexico, University of Denver, and University of Minnesota. He served in the United States Army in 1943-1944, and has been a newspaper reporter and a teacher of English. He currently teaches at San Francisco State College. He has contributed to *Negro Digest*, the *Nation*, the *American Scholar*, *Commentary*, and other magazines. Another novel, *Something About a Soldier*, is scheduled for publication in the autumn of 1957.

BOOKS: *Trumpet to the World*, 1946; *City of Discontent*, 1952; *The Southpaw*, 1953; *Bang the Drum Slowly*, 1956; *A Ticket for a Seamstitch*, 1957.

GRANVILLE HICKS was born in Exeter, New Hampshire, in 1901, was educated in the public schools of New Hampshire and Massachusetts, and was graduated from Harvard, *summa cum laude*, in 1923. He has taught at Smith College, Harvard, Rensselaer Polytechnic Institute, and the New School for Social Research. He was an editor of the *New Masses* from 1934 to 1939, and has been literary consultant to the *New Leader* since 1951. He has held Guggenheim and Rockefeller fellowships.

BOOKS: *The Great Tradition*, 1933; *John Reed*, 1936; *I Like America*, 1938; *Figures of Transition*, 1939; *The First to Awaken* (with Richard M. Bennett), 1940; *Only One Storm*, 1942; *Behold Trouble*, 1944; *Small Town*, 1946; *There Was a Man in Our Town*, 1952; *Where We Came Out*, 1954.

WRIGHT MORRIS was born in Central City, Nebraska, in 1910, and, as he has said, the influence of the plains is strong in his work. The latter part of his boyhood was spent in Chicago. He attended Pomona College, but left without graduating to travel in Europe. An expert photographer, he has published two books, *The Inhabitants* and *The Home Place*, in which pictures and text, running parallel courses, supplement one another. *The Field of Vision* received the National Book Award in fiction for 1956. Another novel, *Love Among the Cannibals*, was published in the summer of 1957.

BOOKS: *My Uncle Dudley*, 1942; *The Man Who Was There*, 1945; *The Inhabitants*, 1946; *The Home Place*, 1948; *The World in the Attic*, 1949; *Man and Boy*, 1950; *The Works of Love*, 1951;

The Deep Sleep, 1953; *The Huge Season,* 1954; *The Field of Vision,* 1956.

FLANNERY O'CONNOR was born in Savannah, Georgia, in 1925. She was graduated from the Georgia State College for Women, and took her master's degree at State University of Iowa. She lives near Milledgeville, Georgia, and is writing her second novel. Her stories have been published in many magazines, and one of them received first prize in the O. Henry Memorial Award for 1956.

BOOKS: *Wise Blood,* 1952; *A Good Man Is Hard to Find,* 1955.

HARVEY SWADOS was born in Buffalo in 1920, and was graduated from the University of Michigan in 1940. Although he was already determined to become a writer, he decided to support himself by a variety of jobs in order to broaden his experience. He worked in aircraft factories, served in the Merchant Marine, and after the war was employed as a census taker, researcher, publicity writer, and factory hand. In 1956-1957 he was a lecturer at the Writers' Workshop of the State University of Iowa. Although he had published many short stories, book reviews, and articles on popular culture, his first novel did not appear until 1955. He has completed a book of related short stories, entitled *On the Line,* to be published by Atlantic-Little, Brown, and is working on another novel. He has a *Hudson Review* Fellowship in fiction for 1957-1958.

BOOK: *Out Went the Candle,* 1955.

JESSAMYN WEST was born in Indiana but has spent most of her life in California. She attended Whittier College in that state, and has also studied in England and at the University of California. Her first book was a collection of sketches portraying the life of a family of Quakers in Indiana at the time of the Civil War, and her second was a script for an opera based on the life of Audubon. She has contributed many short stories to the *New Yorker* and other magazines. Her most recent book, *To See the Dream*, deals with her experiences and her reflections during the filming of *The Friendly Persuasion*.

BOOKS: *The Friendly Persuasion*, 1945; *Mirror for the Sky*, 1948; *The Witch Diggers*, 1951; *Cress Delahanty*, 1953; *Love, Death, and the Ladies' Drill Team*, 1955; *To See the Dream*, 1957.